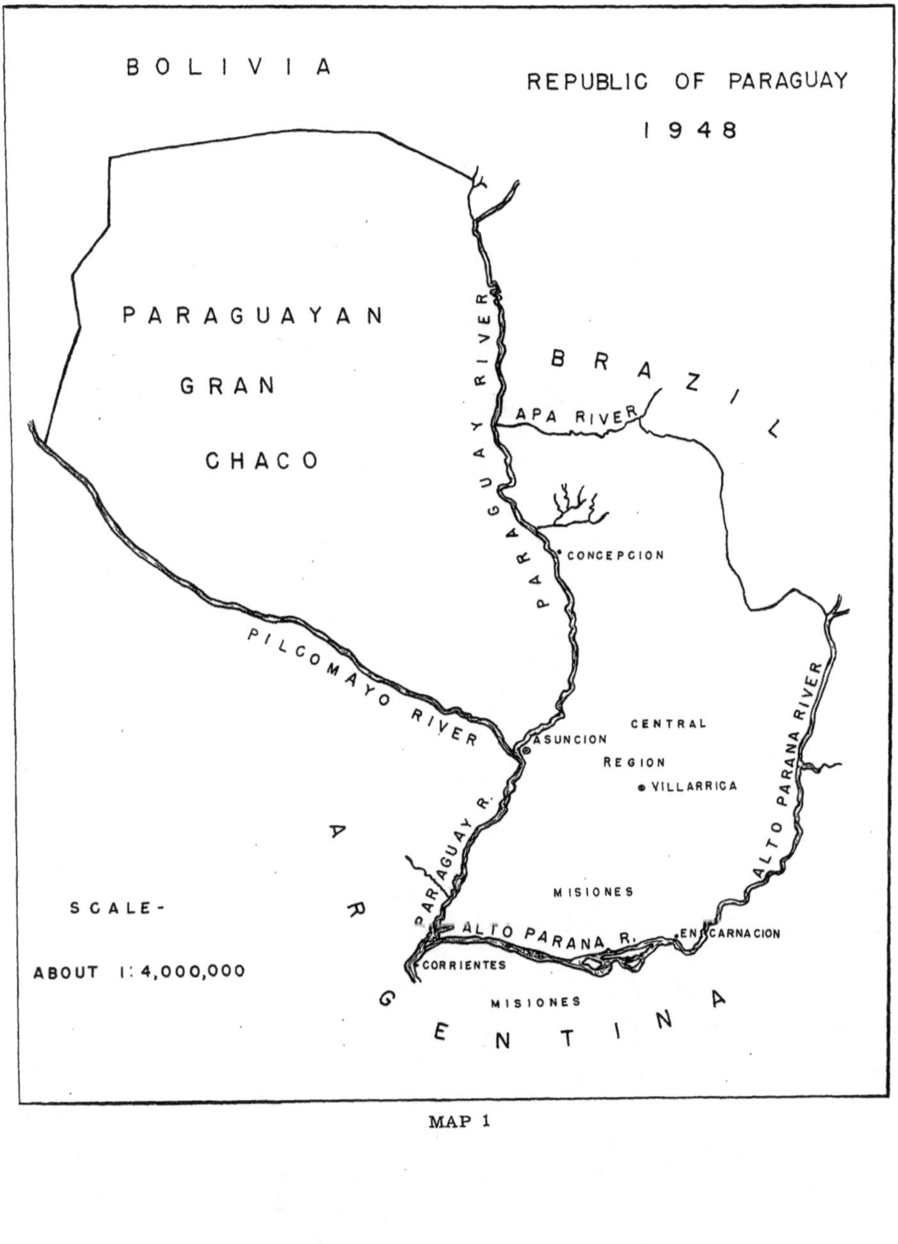
BOLIVIA
REPUBLIC OF PARAGUAY
1948
PARAGUAYAN
GRAN
CHACO
PARAGUAY RIVER
BRAZIL
APA RIVER
CONCEPCION
PILCOMAYO RIVER
ASUNCION
CENTRAL
REGION
VILLARRICA
ALTO PARANA RIVER
PARAGUAY R.
ARGENTINA
MISIONES
SCALE-
ABOUT 1:4,000,000
ALTO PARANA R.
ENCARNACION
CORRIENTES
MISIONES

MAP 1

ANTHROPOLOGICAL PAPERS

MUSEUM OF ANTHROPOLOGY, UNIVERSITY OF MICHIGAN

No. 9

Spanish-Guarani Relations in Early Colonial Paraguay

by

ELMAN R. SERVICE

ANN ARBOR

UNIVERSITY OF MICHIGAN PRESS, 1954

ISBN (print): 978-1-949098-34-1
ISBN (ebook): 978-1-951519-58-2

Browse all of our books at sites.lsa.umich.edu/archaeology-books.

Order our books from the University of Michigan Press at www.press.umich.edu.

For permissions, questions, or manuscript queries, contact Museum publications by email at ummapubs@umich.edu or visit the Museum website at lsa.umich.edu/ummaa.

Composition and Lithoprinting by
BRAUN-BRUMFIELD, Inc.
Ann Arbor, Mich.

CONTENTS

SPANISH-GUARANÍ RELATIONS IN EARLY COLONIAL PARAGUAY

INTRODUCTION

Paraguay is notable for the extent to which the racial and linguistic heritage of the native Guaraní Indians remains to characterize the modern nation. Except for the basically pure Indian population of the Paraguayan Gran Chaco, the million or more people of Paraguay proper are mainly descended from the early Spanish colonists who intermarried with Guaraní women. In the absence of adequate descriptions of Paraguayan culture, the extent of the Guaraní contribution to modern habits and customs is not known, but their language is still spoken more commonly than Spanish.[1]

The racial and social amalgamation of Spaniards and aborigines began very early in the colonial period. Since that time isolation, the slow pace of commercial and industrial development, and the economic ruin following the war against the Triple Alliance have tended to preserve essential features of the colonial patterns. It would seem, therefore, that any attempt to understand or explain the culture of modern Paraguay must take special account of the nature of the mutual adjustment between the Spanish colonists and the indigenous Guaraní Indians during the early phases of their association.

Spanish-Guaraní relations are usually described by modern historians as having been amicable from the period of their first contact.[2] Some authors also have pointed out the importance of this factor in determining subsequent cultural developments in Paraguay. Arcos, for example, said: "The rule of Irala [the most important figure during the

[1]Métraux, 1948, p. 77; Steward, 1945, p. 298; James, 1942, pp. 266-67.

[2]James, 1942, pp. 266-67; Gandía, 1939, pp. 33-34, 47, 58-60; Washburn, 1871, 1:29, 57-58; Pereyra, 1920-27, 4:44; Rubio, 1942, p. 181.

earliest colonial period] is significant on account of the relations which he established between the Spaniards and the Indians, which were of such a nature as in a large measure to determine the character of the later population of Paraguay."[3] Washburn stated: "It was a constant endeavor of Irala to level all distinctions between the Europeans and Natives, and this he effected in a great measure by encouraging his countrymen to take the brown daughters of the forest for wives, to learn their language and conform to their customs in matters not of essential importance . . . . Thus the government and policy of Irala permanently fixed the character, social and political, of the people."[4]

Despite the fact that several authors have pointed out that early relations of Spaniards and aborigines in Paraguay were unusual and that they were important in determining the characteristic development of the later culture, there has been no adequate description of these relations with a view to explaining the accultural situation in the colonial period. Several writers have noted the problems with which this study is concerned, and speculative answers have been given, but there is nowhere a work devoted to a fuller elucidation. Most of the few studies of Paraguayan history have focused attention on the men and events of the conquest and on subsequent political phenomena of the colonial period, but the social and cultural circumstances have been relatively ignored.

Obviously, all modern peoples of Latin America are highly acculturated, whether one judges from the point of view of the changes in sixteenth-century Spanish culture due to contact with local indigenous groups, or from the standpoint of the modification of American Indian cultures due to Spanish domination. Probably the greatest present weakness in our studies of modern Latin American peoples is the general lack of information on the cultural changes which were concomitant with the mutual adjustments of the Iberian and native peoples.[5] Nearly all the Latin American countries possess a richly documented colonial history from which these important changes can be learned or inferred,

[3]Quoted in Moses, 1898, p. 194.

[4]Washburn, 1871, 1:57-58.

[5]Steward, 1943, p. 22.

but so far the only beginnings which have been made in this field are a recent study of the Quechua in the colonial period in Peru by Kubler,[6] and La Farge's short essay on the Maya.[7]

The study which these pages introduce can be considered an attempt to contribute toward an understanding of the culture history of Paraguay by focusing attention on Spanish-Guaraní relations during the critical, early colonial period. In reviewing this situation the study will concern itself with three related aims: (1) to describe the nature of the Spanish-Guaraní relations during their formative period, with particular emphasis on those aspects which seem unusual or unique in the Spanish colonies in the New World; (2) to appraise the total situation in an effort to determine those circumstances of the conquest and colonization which help to explain why these relations took unusual forms; and (3) to describe the Spanish-Guaraní acculturation in terms of the influences of these circumstances and relations.

The means of exploitation and control of indigenous populations which the Spaniards employed in different parts of the New World were similar in their conception and intent. They were, however, often modified by local conditions of geography, kinds of available wealth, and the type of native population. The encomienda, a system of administration of conquered populations which had its historical roots in Spain, was the colonial institution which, more than any other, systematized and patterned the relationship between the conquerors and the natives. For this reason the present study of Spanish-Indian relations in Paraguay must be devoted mainly to an analysis of the encomienda. Inasmuch as the laws regulating this institution were promulgated by the Spanish King and his Council of the Indies, they were usually formulated to apply to all of the Spanish possessions in the New World. Any important exceptions in the application of these rules in Paraguay, as compared to other areas, should, therefore, emphasize and make explicit those features which were unusual in the relationships of Spaniards and Paraguayan Indians.

[6]Kubler, 1946.

[7]La Farge, 1940.

Philip II's cedula of 1571 defines the encomienda in the following fashion: "The encomienda is a right granted by Royal Grace to the deserving of the Indies to receive and collect for themselves the tributes of the Indians that shall be given them in trust, for their life and the life of one heir . . . with the charge of looking after the spiritual and temporal welfare of the Indians and of dwelling in and defending the Provinces where they are given them in trust and of doing homage and making personal oath to fulfill all this."[8]

In general, the encomienda, as conceived by the Crown laws, took the following form:[9] the Indians were "reduced" to a settled town life whereby they could be more easily controlled, "protected," and taught the Christian doctrine by the Spanish encomendero. The encomendero was compensated for these responsibilities by a fixed yearly tribute or tax to be paid him by mature male Indians. The monetary value of the tribute was fixed, but it could be paid by equivalent values in crops. Personal service in lieu of tribute was expressly forbidden by the Crown. The Indians lived "politically" (governed in Spanish fashion) under legal municipal officers who were native members of their own towns. When the period during which the encomienda belonged to a Spaniard ended, the vacant encomienda reverted to the Crown, the Indians were considered vassals of the King and otherwise "free," and the period of tutelage was over. The general rule was for the encomienda to last for the lifetime of the first encomendero and one heir, although there were many special cases in which this period was lengthened.

The Crown and its representatives had a great deal of difficulty in restricting the use of the Indians as a labor force. After the disastrous effects of Spanish exploitation of natives of the West Indies had been forcefully brought

[8]Solórzano, 1930, 1:237; also translated and quoted by Simpson, 1929, on unnumbered page following title page; and by Barber, 1932, p. 17.

[9]The general meaning of the encomienda in the New World is not discussed here in any detail because there are many excellent works which deal with its general historical and legalistic aspects. See the following studies which appear in English: Simpson, 1929, 1934, 1938a, 1940; Barber, 1932; Hanke, 1935; Zavala, 1943. These are the works consulted most often in the preparation of these pages.

to the attention of the King,[10] decrees forbidding personal service in lieu of tribute were repeatedly issued. Zavala showed that the enforcement of the royal decree of 1549 effectively marked the end of the encomienda as a labor institution in Mexico and Peru. From that time all tributes were to be paid in money, produce, or native wares.[11]

Under this prohibition the colonists had considerable difficulty in obtaining labor, for the Indians, because of their habits and customs, did not freely hire themselves out as wage laborers. In Mexico and Peru the difficulty was eventually solved by the utilization of corvée labor for work on certain projects "for the public good." In Mexico this institution was called the "cuatequil" or "repartimiento," and in Peru, the "mita." In both regions it was modeled on an aboriginal system of labor levies for public works. Under the Spaniards the Indian laborers received a fixed daily wage, and the hours and conditions of labor were regulated by law. The Indians did not work for their encomenderos, but on projects selected by public officials. This system, which was characteristic of the latter half of the sixteenth century in Mexico and Peru, thus had an important effect on the encomienda. The Spanish encomendero began to lose some of his control over his Indians because their labor was regulated by public authorities independently of his wishes.[12]

There was also another important labor institution developing in Mexico, Central America, and the Andean region during the early colonial period. Some Spanish colonists had been successful in inducing Indian families to remain permanently on their estates as wage laborers. In these areas such workers were known as naborías or laborías. Eventually, the Spanish landowner advanced money and goods to these Indians, so that, being legally bound to repay the debt, they were forced into permanent residence on the land. This type of debt-peonage, as distinct from both the encomienda and the mita, was the true precursor of the hacienda system of later times.[13]

[10]Father Bartólome de las Casas was the most prominent of the ecclesiastics who protested against the Spanish colonists' treatment of the West Indian aborigenes. Las Casas, 1909.

[11]Zavala, 1943, p. 85.

[12]*Ibid.*, pp. 94-97.

[13]*Ibid.*, p. 99.

It has been noted that the Spanish Crown's concern over mistreatment of the Indians resulted in increasing prohibitions of the exploitation of their labor by Spaniards. One means of saving the Indians from exploitation was to make the encomienda regulations increasingly rigid and to make Spanish contact with the encomienda Indians as remote as possible. The encomendero was to teach them the faith and protect them, but he was not allowed their personal service even if it were voluntary. From time to time many other restrictions designed to protect the Indians were instituted: laws were passed to prevent Spaniards from living in Indian towns, merchants were not allowed to remain more than three days, and the encomendero himself could not stay more than one night.[14]

An important aspect of these protective measures is that they tended in effect to preserve the original culture of the Indians, though in somewhat modified form, much as the reservation system in the United States tended to keep a certain kind of modified Indian culture alive and functioning. It is important to note here that the regulations governing the encomienda in Paraguay never acquired the rigidity found in other Spanish colonies.

The postconquest acculturation periods, as outlined by La Farge, Steward, and Kubler for other Spanish-American areas, were condensed into a remarkably short space of time in Paraguay. La Farge suggested the following periods for the acculturation of the Maya: Conquest Period, 1524-1600; Colonial Indian, 1600-1720; First Transition, 1720-1800; Recent Indian I, 1800-1880; Recent Indian II, 1800--.[15] Steward has divided the acculturation history of the tribes of the east slope of the Andes in Ecuador, Peru, and Bolivia into three main periods: (1) Exploration and Conquest, 1532-1643, a period of little effect on the Indians; (2) Mission or Colonial Period, 1630-1830; and (3) the National Period, 1830—.[16] Kubler has divided the acculturation of the Quechua into five main historical phases:

[14]Simple humanitarianism was not the only motive behind the Crown laws which protected the Indians and limited the power of the encomenderos. These laws were also partly a result of the attempt to limit feudal privileges of potentially powerful individuals in order to centralize power in Spain. See Simpson's statement of this, 1946, p. 50.

[15]La Farge, 1940, pp. 290-91.

[16]Steward, 1946-50, 3:510-14.

(1) Conquest Quechua, 1532-1572; (2) Early Colonial Quechua, 1572-ca. 1650; (3) Mature Colonial Quechua, ca. 1650-ca. 1750; (4) Late Colonial Quechua, ca. 1750-1821; (5) Republican Quechua, 1821--.[17] In all of these suggested sequences the writers have sketched irregular, sporadic periods of cumulative absorption of Indian culture into a European form, an acculturation, which, though increasing from period to period, is not complete even at the present time.

In Paraguay the postconquest acculturation of the Guaraní Indians suggests the following divisions: (1) The Exploratory Phase, 1537-1556; (2) The Transitional Phase, 1556-1580; (3) The Colonial Phase, 1580-1812. The Exploratory Phase began with the founding of Asunción and concluded with the establishment of the encomienda system by Governor Irala in 1556. During this time Asunción was a base for explorations into the Chaco toward the Andes in search of mineral wealth. No systematic attempt was made to adapt the Indians to a colonial way of life because the Spaniards regarded their occupation of Asunción as merely temporary. They formed a military alliance with the Guaraní and used the Indian women as concubines and servants. Guaraní acculturation was thus informal, expedient, and confined to the villages near Asunción. Irala's grants of encomiendas in 1556 initiated a period of transition from this local situation to the full expression of the Paraguayan encomienda system, which in a generation or so brought the more remote Guaraní Indians into a regulated system of control and exploitation. During this period mestizos assumed an important role as encomenderos and founders of new towns and encomiendas, and by about 1580 the change from the exploratory period to the period of stable encomiendas had been effected in all essentials. From this time no large new groups of Indians were subjugated, nor were there really any permanent changes at any point in the subsequent history of the colonial institutions. The true Paraguayan was, and is, a mestizo with a distinctive national language and culture, the basis of which was formed before the end of the sixteenth century.

[17]Kubler, 1946, pp. 340-54.

For the present purpose the scope of the problem here outlined must be limited both temporally and geographically. This study is therefore restricted to the period from 1537, the first settling of Paraguay, to 1620. The year 1620 is chosen as the terminal date for two reasons. In 1611 Francisco de Alfaro promulgated a series of ordinances which were to cause certain temporary changes in Spanish-Indian relations, but by 1620 his ordinances had been modified to conform to the requirements of the Paraguayan economy, and thereafter no important legal changes disturbed the encomienda until 1812, when the system was abolished. In 1617 the King of Spain divided the original province of Río de la Plata into two parts. Paraguay, with Asunción as the capital, became a separate government, and Buenos Aires became the capital of the rest of the La Plata area. This served further to reduce the importance of Paraguay and to isolate it from the rest of the world even more than before. The period of most rapid cultural change and development occurred during the early phase of Spanish settlement. After about 1580 a period of slower growth and adaptation to local circumstances began. Alfaro's attempt to institute reforms in 1611 is important to consider because his failure reveals the nature of the Paraguayan situation and indicates that the cultural adjustment by that time had great stability. After the division of the province into two parts nothing of great cultural significance occurred during the remainder of the colonial period.[18] From this point of view the years before 1620 constituted the formative period in Paraguayan postconquest culture history.

So far as area is concerned, this study will not be concerned with the Gran Chaco, nor with the region of the Jesuit missions. The Chaco was not settled successfully by Spaniards during the colonial period. It was a difficult area geographically and was populated by intransigent tribes whose subjugation appeared to be virtually impossible. The presence of these warlike tribes had important consequences in strengthening the early Spanish-Guaraní alliance, but their culture did not enter significantly into the compound

[18] As late as 1780 the "Protector of the Indians" of Paraguay made a full report on ecomiendas which could easily be a description of encomiendas in 1620. See Pino Manrique: 1780.

which became Paraguayan culture, and to the present day the Chaco remains culturally distinct from what is considered "Paraguay proper."

The well-known "Jesuit Empire" of thirty mission towns was situated mainly in the Alto Paraná River basin, first in Brazil, from about 1609, and later mostly in the present territory of Misiones until the Jesuit order was expelled from the New World in 1767. It would seem that the cultural influence of these missions has often been exaggerated, as their area was remote from the central one of Spanish settlement, and the missions were further sealed off from contact with the rest of Paraguay by design of the mission fathers.

This is not to say that the Jesuits in Paraguay were insignificant in other respects, however, for they did figure prominently in the political history of colonial Paraguay. Their missions were very important in providing a strategic buffer against the expanding Portuguese empire in Brazil. Eventually, they were allowed to arm their Indians to counter Brazilian raids into their territory, and this military power became influential in Paraguayan internal affairs, as the Jesuits could hold a balance of power by supporting one political faction against another. Their political importance naturally made them the subject of a considerable body of historical literature.

The controversial "communistic" social order of the missions also has attracted so much attention that many writers have entered the argument over the merits or deficiencies of their social scheme. The resulting abundance of source material and secondary works has made the "Jesuit State" by far the best known aspect of Paraguayan history; consequently, there is a tendency to overrate its influence as a determinant in the formation of Paraguayan national culture.

The area where the missions were established was so remote and inaccessible from Asunción that most of the trade was necessarily by river traffic with Buenos Aires rather than with Asunción. The jealousy of the government at Asunción and the occasional political strife further served to restrict intercourse between Paraguayans and mission Indians. The acculturation of Indians by the Jesuits was thereby limited exclusively to the Indians who actually inhabited the mission towns.

Within these towns the Indians were very closely supervised and regimented by the mission fathers. Religious teachings were, naturally, greatly emphasized. Economic affairs were strictly communal: work in the community fields was a collective enterprise, and the herds and granaries were publicly owned and the products equally distributed. The Indians and their families all dressed identically and lived in identical communal dwellings. The only socially distinctive people were the Jesuits themselves, who functioned as teachers and "benevolent dictators."

When the Jesuits were expelled, the missions began to deteriorate. Control was divided between Franciscans and lay administrators, who apparently made no successful attempts to prevent the invasion of fortune hunters and unscrupulous traders. The Indians had been so closely supervised by the Jesuit fathers in the communal life of the missions that they were unable to cope with the outside world. Rapid demoralization occurred, and most of the Indians abandoned the missions and either retreated to the forests to survive marginally or were forced to work for Spanish encomenderos. Those who remained in the missions underwent many hardships during the rest of their history, and in 1848 the missions which were still within the shrunken boundaries of Paraguay were abolished and the Indians were forced to live as Paraguayan citizens.

It seems likely, then, that although the presence of the missions is of historical interest, their acculturation of the mission Indians had little permanent effect on the culture of the general population of Paraguay. During the period when the missions existed they were sealed off from the rest of Paraguay by design and by circumstances, and after the Jesuits were expelled the surviving Indians were forced to become adjusted to a Paraguayan cultural configuration, the essential patterns of which had long been in existence as a product of a radically different kind of acculturation.[19]

Sources of data for the present study include published and unpublished collections of documents used in conjunction with the few modern studies available. Documentary

[19]The most important source for this material on the Jesuits is Hernández, 1913.

material on Paraguay is not plentiful, and, as Barber has pointed out in the Introduction to her study, Indian Labor in the Spanish Colonies,[20] a student of Spanish-Indian relations is confronted with grave difficulties because of the controversial character of most of the writing which relates to this subject. The question of Spanish colonization in the Americas is nearly always approached with a spirit of passionate defense or condemnation of Spain's colonial policy.[21]

Some of the best sources of information among the published documents are the various ordinances relating to Spanish-Indian relations in Paraguay, provided they are used with caution. A law prohibiting a certain action may mean that the action is thenceforth effectively prevented, or it may be merely evidence that the action is commonplace. Laws, therefore, cannot be depended upon as straightforward sources of data, for their meaning at any given time must be inferred by a consideration of the specific circumstances.

The following groups of ordinances supply an important amount of the data to be employed:

1. One set of ordinances of Domingo Martínez de Irala, 1556, on the occasion of the first encomienda grants in Paraguay.[22]

2. Forty-eight ordinances by Governor Ramírez de Velasco, 1597. These ordinances are particularly valuable because they describe each situation quite fully before ordering the precise remedy.[23]

3. Twenty-nine ordinances by Governor Hernandarias de Saavedra, 1603, which are similarly full of descriptive material.[24]

4. Eighty-six ordinances by Francisco de Alfaro, 1611, are particularly valuable for several reasons. Most of his ordinances make it clear that important laws made by

[20]Barber, 1932, pp. 1-16.

[21]The polemic nature of the writings on this subject has continued from the time of Bartólome de las Casas' book, Destruction of the the Indies, first published in 1552, to modern times. See Simpson's analysis of this problem, 1929.

[22]Irala: 1556a.

[23]Ramírez de Velasco: 1597.

[24]Hernandarias de Saavedra: 1603.

the governors cited above were ineffective. Alfaro's own ordinances are complete and detailed down to very specific points. They aroused such a storm of protest that it is possible to gauge their effectiveness by reading the various documents which discuss and object to particular provisions of his laws. It is fortunate for modern historians that he even attempted to initiate these changes, for otherwise the documentary literature would be very meager on many points of interest in this period.[25]

Only paraphrased extracts of the pertinent ordinances will be presented in this study, as the ordinances are all easily available in full in the publications cited.

Unpublished copies of manuscripts in the Manuel E. Gondra collection, recently purchased from the Gondra family by the University of Texas, constitute another important source of data. Since the collection is not finally catalogued and described at the date of this writing, it is possible that some of the descriptive titles listed in the bibliography may eventually be changed. The manuscript number is given in each case, however, in order to provide an accurate check.

Unless otherwise stated, I have made all translations quoted in the text. In the case of unpublished material, an exact, untranslated copy of the cited passage will be quoted in a footnote. In the case of easily available published sources, translations or paraphrasings have been made without including a copy of the original statement, except in cases where an interpretation might be questioned.

The form used for footnotes—and also for the bibliography—departs from established procedure to some extent. The short form, citing the author's last name and date of publication of the work, is used for all published books and articles in accordance with current usage. For letters and documentary sources published in modern collections, or published as appendices to modern works, the reference indicates the original author's name and the date of the writing of the document, rather than the modern publication date. In these cases the author's name and the date are separated by a colon instead of a comma (e.g., Irala: 1556). Thus, primary source materials are distinguishable from secondary works, which appear in the usual

[25]Alfaro: 1611; Consejo de Indias: 1618.

form (Gandía, 1939, p. 54). Unpublished documents from the Gondra collection are identified by their catalog numbers (Gondra MS 209), to distinguish them from published sources and to ensure identification.

Grateful acknowledgment is made to the Wenner-Gren Foundation for Anthropological Research, New York City, for the grant-in-aid which made possible the research in the Manuel E. Gondra collection of documents and rare books in the Latin American Library of the University of Texas.

I am also grateful to the late Professor Charles Hackett, director of the University of Texas Institute of Latin American Studies, and to the University of Texas Library staff for permission to study the Gondra collection. Professor Pablo Max Insfran, Miss Nettie Lee Benson, and Mr. Robert Florstedt were especially helpful to my research in that university.

Colleagues at Columbia University were most helpful during the preparation of the manuscript. Professor Julian H. Steward was very generous with important suggestions and criticisms during all stages of the writing, and I should also like to thank Professors William Duncan Strong and Charles Wagley for their careful reading of the manuscript.

I. THE ABORIGINAL AND HISTORICAL BACKGROUND

The Aboriginal Culture of the Guaraní Indians[26]

At the time of the Spanish exploration of the La Plata region, Guaraní-speaking Indians occupied a large area extending from the Atlantic coast westward to the Paraguay River, covering much of the present-day Rio Grande do Sul, Paraná, Misiones Territory, and virtually all of Paraguay east of the Gran Chaco. This part of Paraguay and the Paraná Basin to the east were occupied almost exclusively by Guaraní.

[26] Alfred Métraux's article in the Handbook of South American Indians is the most modern account of the Guaraní. The data contained in the present section are taken entirely from this source unless otherwise stated. Métraux, 1948.

The Paraguayan Gran Chaco, a very flat, often flooded, alluvial plain, was a difficult area in which to gain subsistence and was populated mainly by warlike non-Guaraní tribes. The rest of Paraguay, to the east of the Paraguay River, presented an entirely different aspect. Well watered, but also relatively well drained in comparison with the Chaco, the land was favorable to the horticulture of the Guaraní. This became the area of primary Spanish settlement. The central part of this area is a hilly, savanna-like land, with about fifty inches of annual rainfall and with seasonal temperature changes similar to those in southern Florida. The eastern third of the country is a plateau varying from one thousand to two thousand feet in altitude. Somewhat greater rainfall and lower temperatures in this region have resulted in a cover of deciduous forests. A warm climate, moderate rainfall, and the combination of fertile soil, grasslands, and forest inspired Preston James and others to call Paraguay a natural paradise.[27]

There are no trustworthy reports of the original Guaraní population among the early sources. Steward's recent estimate of two hundred thousand for the Paraguayan and south Brazilian Guaraní is probably the most reliable modern estimate. He gave a population density of roughly twenty-eight persons per one hundred square kilometers in central Paraguay, with thirty-three per one hundred square kilometers along the Alto Paraná River.[28] In reading early accounts of the conquest one receives the impression that the Guaraní were concentrated more thickly along the Paraguay River in the region near Asunción than in the interior. This seems probable when one considers the aboriginal tendency to concentrate along large rivers.

Guaraní culture was roughly similar to the generic culture type called Tropical Forest in the classification used in the Handbook of South American Indians,[29] and more specifically similar to that of the Tupí-speaking tribes such as the Tupinambá of the Brazilian east coast and the Chiriguano of eastern Bolivia. These two groups are closely related linguistically to the Guaraní, and probably all

[27]James, 1942, p. 268. Most of the geographic description is based on material from James's book.

[28]Steward, 1946-50, 5:659, 662, Map 16.

[29]Ibid., Vol. 3.

had been more closely associated with one another geographically before the Spanish conquest. Their cultural similarity is so great that it must be assumed that they had migrated from a common homeland not many years before the arrival of the Spaniards.

Subsistence activities were based on widespread Tropical Forest agricultural techniques. Since there was no irrigation or fertilization of cultivated fields, every two or three years the fields had to be abandoned because of soil exhaustion. The usual tropical plants were grown, sweet manioc and maize being the most important staples. Several kinds of sweet potatoes, beans, peanuts, and pumpkins were also cultivated. The Muscovy duck was the only domesticated animal, and most meat, therefore, was obtained by hunting. Tapir and deer were the largest game animals. Fishing and gathering wild products, such as honey, pine nuts in some regions, and palm-tree products, were important supplementary subsistence activities. The Guaraní also cultivated several nonfood plants, such as gourds, calabash trees, tobacco, and cotton.

The digging stick was the basic agricultural tool, and the bow and arrow the important hunting weapon. For cooking, pottery was used and probably green bamboo joints; meat was roasted on a spit or grill of green sticks. The wooden mortar was used for food grinding. Large clay pots were used as chicha beer containers and as funeral urns. Twilled baskets were made, and loom weaving of cotton was practiced.

The villages were usually composed of about four to eight large, thatched, communal buildings, each housing the several families forming one patrilineal lineage. Sometimes as many as sixty families lived in the same building, and often a whole village inhabited a single house.[30] The villages were surrounded by double or triple stockades and a series of moats. Inside the building vertical posts separated the quarters of the individual families. Furniture consisted mostly of hammocks for sleeping and four-legged benches. These villages were moved every few years as the fields in the vicinity became exhausted.

The social unit of importance was the large extended patrilineal lineage which occupied the communal house. Each unit had a headman or chief, and if the village was

[30]Techo, 1744-46, pp. 717-18.

composed of more than one lineage, these chiefs were probably subservient to a village chief, as among the Tupinambá. Evidence from the seventeenth century suggests that shamans may also have acted as chiefs, though this was perhaps a result of tendencies inherent in the post-Columbian acculturative situation, wherein shamans often came to have exaggerated political powers because of their prominence in nativistic movements.

The Guaraní chief's power over his subjects was limited compared to that wielded by chiefs in the higher cultures of the Andes and circum-Caribbean areas. Guaraní society was not class structured with a hereditary hierarchy of chiefs whose authority extended over great numbers of conquered or federated villages. Archeological evidence from the area does not indicate any particular pomp or ceremony connected with the burial of privileged persons, and chieftainship was not strictly hereditary. An eloquent man distinguished in war might succeed to chieftainship instead of the son of a former chief although an elder son would probably be favored.

The chief's crops were planted and harvested by the members of his community. Chiefs or important people commonly had several wives or concubines, the numbers of which were rough gauges of their prestige and status. The village chief in a multilineage village would normally have more status than the heads of the separate kinship units of the village. Some chiefs seem to have been able to extend their influence over several villages, but there was, as a rule, no widespread pattern of confederation or conquest. To the extent that the position of these leaders was hereditary, the Guaraní may be said to have had a status system tending toward a hereditary class system.

There was no hereditary priestly class or temple cult. The shaman was the only religious functionary. His political power varied with his ability to acquire prestige and inspire fear, but the normal functions of a shaman were only to cure disease and perform miraculous feats. Anyone could become a shaman who possessed the necessary personal qualifications. The lack of power of the leaders, whether chiefs or shamans, continually impressed the

Spaniards, who often referred to the general anarchy and lack of leadership.[31]

The system of kinship nomenclature was probably of the Dakota or bilateral type.[32] This system is usually correlated with an extended family or lineage type of social organization rather than with clan organization. Relationship terms are extended so that father's brothers and mother's sisters are termed "father" and "mother," cousins are called by the terms for siblings, and a male's brother's children and a female's sister's children are "sons" and "daughters." Terminology for grandparents and grandchildren is extended to include all people of the proper generations who are considered relatives. Such a system would probably embrace from fifty to one hundred people, on the average, though there were undoubtedly larger lineages. The fact that some communal dwellings have been described as housing as many as sixty families must mean that some lineages might include as many as three hundred people.

Information on Guaraní marriage customs is scanty, but it seems that the preferred marriage was between cross-cousins or between a girl and her maternal uncle. Polygyny was common, both sororal and with a mother and her daughters. The Jesuits had a great deal of difficulty in persuading the Indians to give up polygyny, as it was apparently important for social reasons. Some chiefs were said to have had from fifteen to thirty wives.

Guaraní warfare was probably defensive in the main, since their territory was ringed by aggressive tribes who had preyed on them to such an extent that, on the arrival of the Spanish explorers, the Guaraní eagerly allied themselves with the equally hard-pressed Europeans for greater security.

To the west of the Guaraní, across the Paraguay River, and to the north such tribes as the Guaycurú, the Toba, Payaguá, Pilagá, and Lengua were persistent raiders even

[31]For example, see Governor Irala's statement of this characteristic. Lafuente Machain, 1939, p. 42; Dorantes: 1553, p. 486.

[32]Evidence from historical records and from several modern Tupí-speaking tribes indicates that the Dakota system was widespread among Tupían groups. The only exceptional characteristic of the Tupían system is that cross-cousins as well as parallel cousins were called "brother" and "sister." See Wagley and Galvão, 1946.

after a long period of Spanish colonization. To the south and southeast, in Argentina and Uruguay, were the Querandí and Charrua plains nomads, whom the Spanish settlers of those areas found bellicose. To the east were non-Guaraní tribes--usually called "Tupí" by the chroniclers--who raided the Guaraní of the province of Guayrá. During much of the colonial period Brazilian slave raiders, the famous "Paulistas" or "Mamelucos," raided the same region.

As far as the effect of this situation on the initial Spanish-Guaraní alliance is concerned, it was the Guaycurú and Payaguá who were of most significance in the region of the first Spanish settlement. At the time of the arrival of the Spaniards, the Guaraní living in the vicinity of Asunción along the Paraguay River had great difficulty in defending themselves from these two Chaco tribes.

In the province of Guayrá the "Tupí," who were encouraged or pushed by the Portuguese to make incursions into Paraguay, and the Portuguese themselves were the important factors in encouraging Spanish-Guaraní co-operation, the Guaraní for their own safety, and the Spaniards in order to consolidate and hold as much territory as they possibly could against their Portuguese rivals.

Historical Sketch of Spanish Colonization in Paraguay from 1537 to 1620

The first explorations of the Río de la Plata region were inspired by false beliefs that the region was rich in gold and silver and that the river would provide an easy route to Peru. When Sebastian Cabot stopped on the Brazilian coast at Santa Catarina in 1526, he encountered a few European survivors of the Solís expedition, which had been shipwrecked near that island. They had silver ornaments obtained from the Indians and had heard legends of great wealth to be obtained from the west. Cabot thereupon abandoned his plan to sail to the East Indies and instead sailed up the Paraná and Paraguay rivers as far as the junction of the Pilcomayo, but did not find the source of the silver worn by many of the Indians he encountered. These ornaments had probably come from Peru and Bolivia by aboriginal trade routes.

The reports about this supposedly wealthy region led to the organization of the Pedro de Mendoza expedition, which came to the La Plata from Spain in 1535 and founded a temporary settlement near the present site of Buenos Aires. This expedition originally was composed of about thirteen hundred men and one hundred horses,[33] but lack of food and battles with Charrua and Querandí Indians reduced the numbers considerably before any systematic exploration of the region could be undertaken.

The first attempt by members of the Mendoza expedition to explore farther up the river in search of the "Sierra de la Plata" was made by a group of 170 men under Juán de Ayolas. They sailed up the Paraguay River and crossed the Chaco to eastern Bolivia, but on their return trip in 1538 they were all killed by Payaguá Indians.

Another party of about seventy Spaniards put in at a small bay near the junction of the Paraná and Paraguay rivers in 1537, where they encountered the Guaraní Indians. It was fortunate for the newcomers that the Guaraní, who were hard pressed by the raids of other Indians, chose to receive them as allies rather than as enemies. The Spaniards realized that their own need of allies was very great because of the considerable losses which they had previously suffered in battles with Indians. As a result, an alliance was formed and, farther up the Paraguay River, still in the land of the Guaraní, the fort of Asunción was founded on August 15, 1537.

Asunción soon became the Spanish headquarters and the base from which all further explorations were to be made, since the Spaniards were for the first time settled in a region where the Indians were friendly and useful as servants, food providers, and allies in war. Great care was taken by the Spaniards not to break the customs or wound the sensibilities of the Guaraní.[34] Rubio remarked that the alliance then made between the Guaraní and Spaniards was "a factor of extraordinary importance, without which it would not be possible to explain the action of the

[33]Rubio, 1942, p. 106. This is the most modern and best documented account of the colonization of the Río de la Plata and is therefore the work consulted most often in the preparation of the historical section of this study.

[34]Ibid., p. 154.

latter in Paraguay, for, thanks to this friendship, the conquest was possible."[35]

At this time the assignment of lands and the establishment of encomiendas was not considered because the Spaniards still hoped to find gold and silver mines or Indians with treasure to give in tribute, and they had no intention of forming a permanent settlement. As the name Río de la Plata suggests, this was the land in which it was believed that fabulous wealth could be found.[36] In the absence of encomiendas the Spaniards acquired numbers of Guaraní women, who served not only as wives or concubines, but also as servants and food providers. The relatives of these women also helped provide food and labor for the Spaniards in the same manner in which they customarily provided for the heads of their own lineages. The Guaraní apparently considered this situation a normal consequence of the alliance.

The original leader of the party, Pedro de Mendoza, had died in 1537, and Domingo de Irala became the leader of the remnants of the expedition. In 1541 Irala ordered the small population of Buenos Aires removed to Asunción, leaving the former port abandoned until it was finally refounded in 1580. As Alonso Cabrera, veedor of the province, explained in a letter to Irala, it was necessary to join the two settlements for defense, because there did not remain more than 350 Spaniards in the whole land.[37] The King of Spain, meanwhile, had appointed Alvar Núñez Cabeza de Vaca to take the place of Mendoza. The new governor finally arrived in Asunción in 1542 and took over the leadership of the colony from Irala. Cabeza de Vaca's expedition, the first and only important reinforcement that the young colony was to receive for many years, brought the total number of Spaniards to about six hundred.[38]

[35]Ibid., p. 135. Pereyra also considered the alliance one of the unique features of the colonization of Paraguay and of utmost importance in explaining the subsequent history of the colony. 1920-27, 4:78.

[36]Levene, 1937, p. 17. Levene pointed out in the same passage that the King was interested in the settlement of the region as a bulwark against extension of the Portuguese conquest. This fact was, of course, of less interest to the colonists themselves than acquisition of personal wealth.

[37]Quoted in Gandía, 1932c, p. 89.

[38]Báez, 1926, p. 26. There were subsequent attempts at re-enforcement, notably those of Sanabria and Rasquín, but they ended disastrously.

This was a small number of soldiers for the huge area they hoped to dominate. Asunción was one thousand miles from the mouth of the La Plata, and much of the intervening area was populated by hostile tribes. The fort was especially threatened by a great number of enemies in the nearby Chaco. It is plain that the Spaniards would have been in an untenable position without the aid of the Guaraní Indians.

Numerous co-operative military expeditions were carried out during the first years of the settlement. Under Spanish leadership the Guaraní won a number of victories over their Chaco enemies, the Guaycurú and Payaguá tribes. Spanish prestige grew as a consequence of these military victories, and the Guaraní were conspicuous in all of the large expeditions subsequently undertaken by the Spaniards.

The first really large-scale attempt to use Guaraní military auxiliaries in putting down the warlike Chaco tribes occurred in 1542, when Cabeza de Vaca combined two hundred Spaniards and many more Guaraní into one army. They co-operated successfully, but failed to catch the enemy in a large enough concentration to subdue them with finality.[39] This successful co-operation, however, apparently assured Cabeza de Vaca that the Spaniards could count on enough help to allow him to undertake a large expedition in search of the wealth of the "Sierra de la Plata," and in 1543 he started through the Chaco with four hundred Spaniards and one thousand Guaraní, leaving two hundred Spaniards in Asunción.[40] The expedition penetrated to the province of Chiquitos in eastern Bolivia. Fever, hunger, and wars with the Indians brought the expedition to an inglorious close, and the survivors returned to Asunción a year later no richer than before.

Soon after his return Cabeza de Vaca was imprisoned by Irala and his followers, who kept him in Asunción for nearly a year, after which he was sent to Spain in chains. Irala then resumed his former role as governor of the colony. There is no need to discuss here the relative merits, as governors, of the two rivals, Irala and Cabeza

[39] Rubio, 1942, pp. 183-84.

[40] Ibid., p. 190. This supports the previously cited statement of Báez that after Cabeza de Vaca's arrival there were six hundred Spaniards in Asunción.

de Vaca. Their rivalry and the partisanship of various chroniclers for one or the other are of importance, however, in judging the value of much of the source material on this period for, as so often happened in Spanish-America, accusations and counteraccusations of mistreatment of the Indians were favorite weapons used in carrying on political rivalry. Actually, there is little incontestable evidence that either Cabeza de Vaca or Irala treated the Indians with unusual cruelty. Irala's policies will be fully dealt with in a later section; as for Cabeza de Vaca, Rubio made a good case for his tact in dealing with the natives.[41]

One of the first problems faced by Irala after he took over the leadership was a Guaraní rebellion in 1545, which he put down in a short battle, with the aid of two thousand "loyal" Indians.[42] There is no evidence that this short-lived rebellion was a nativistic, messiah-led movement coming as a consequence of a breakdown of Indian culture. Irala apparently allowed, or the Spaniards took, more liberties with the Indians during the undisciplined period following Irala's coup than had been permitted previously, and this was the Guaraní response to specific abuses. The Spaniards were undoubtedly worried by this demonstration, for Gregorio de Acosta, in this same year, wrote to the King: " . . . the land remains in such danger in all parts that it may be possible that when Your Majesty should want to remedy it, it will be with great difficulty and the greatest conquest of the Ocean Sea will be lost. . . ."[43]

Irala soon brought the Spaniards more closely under his control and published a number of ordinances which relieved the distress of the Guaraní, after which he energetically began to arrange further explorations. Nufrio (or Nuflo) de Châvez, in 1546 and 1547, was sent on small exploratory expeditions, and finally Irala was able to begin his own "Gran Entrada" to the west with 250 soldiers and more than two thousand Indians.[44] Irala arrived at the Andes after great hardships and many battles with the Chaco Indians, only to find that the region had already been

[41] Ibid., pp. 211-13.

[42] Ibid., pp. 220-23.

[43] Acosta: 1545, p. 13.

[44] Rubio, 1942, p. 229.

occupied by Spaniards from Peru. Irala and his men returned to Asunción in 1549, their hopes of wealth from the Sierras destroyed.

In 1553 he organized another expedition to explore the Chaco in search of the "El Dorado" or "Paitatí," of which the Indian legends supposedly told. With 130 Spanish horsemen and some two thousand Guaraní auxiliaries,[45] Irala began the so-called "Mala Entrada," which was as unsuccessful financially as the previous explorations had been.

Up to this time, except for short forays to subdue local tribes, all expeditions were aimed at securing the wealth which was believed to lie to the west. Soon, however, the Spaniards' attention was turned eastward, for several Guaraní chiefs arrived in Asunción from the unexplored province of Guayrá along the Paraná River, to ask aid from the Spaniards against their enemies, the "Tupíes" of Brazil, whom the Portuguese were encouraging to raid the Guaraní. In 1553 Irala headed an expedition to these parts, which was successful in helping the friendly Guaraní defeat the Tupíes.[46] This was the first important expedition which was devoted to consolidation and protection of eastern Paraguay instead of the search for wealth, and, as such, marks the beginning of a significant new trend in events.

In 1556, in accordance with a Crown order, Governor Irala divided the Indians in the vicinity of Asunción into encomiendas and turned the attention of the Spaniards from the fruitless search for wealth to the task of permanently settling the land as true colonists. These grants of encomiendas set up a system which was intended to follow Crown policy, with the exception that the Indians were to serve the encomendero as laborers instead of paying tribute. The encomienda system widened the sphere of influence of the Spaniards and somewhat altered the nature of the relations between the Spaniards and the Indians. During the earlier, more temporary phase of the Spanish occupation, acculturation of the Indians was not purposeful, but was mostly a by-product of an association which grew

[45] Ibid., p. 258. Díaz de Guzmán said it was 4,000 Indians, and in the year 1550. Gandía, in an editor's footnote, corrected these figures to agree with Rubio's. Díaz de Guzmán, 1943, p. 172.

[46] Díaz de Guzmán, 1943, pp. 178-80.

out of exigency. The encomienda, however, was a Spanish institution expressly designed to control the Indians and exploit them, so that Guaraní acculturation became directed to a greater extent and thus tended to be patterned by the form of the system.

As the encomienda became adapted to Paraguayan circumstances, it took on local characteristics and developed into a rather different institution from that which Crown policy had dictated. Not long after 1556 Indians who worked permanently for Spaniards had acquired the name "originarios," whereas those who lived in their own villages but were controlled by Spanish encomenderos were called "mitayos."

Intermarriage of Spaniards and Guaraní continued, and the mestizo offspring soon greatly outnumbered the peninsular Spaniards in Paraguay, as the original Spaniards were not augmented to any extent by immigration from Spain. These mestizo sons of the conquerors had the legal rights of Spaniards, and some of them replaced their fathers as encomenderos of Indians. The mestizo "Spaniards" who did not succeed to the encomiendas of their fathers became important in furthering the settlement of new towns and forming new encomiendas of Indians in the more remote regions of Paraguay.

The Catholic Church did not play an important role in the colonization of central Paraguay, for this region was always notably lacking in ecclesiastics. Typical documents from this period contain complaints of the lack of clerics and the impiety of both the Spanish and Indian residents. It is true, of course, that most of the New World colonies of Spain lacked enough priests and missionaries to convert the natives as rapidly as the Crown desired, but several historians have agreed that in Paraguay the clerics were notably scarce.[47] The consequence of this lack was that Indians were not being converted to Christianity, and the mestizo population continually scandalized the Spaniards by a lack of piety and a disregard for Christian moral standards.

The lack of religious instruction of Indians and the illegality of their exploitation by the Paraguayans finally attracted the attention of the Spanish Council of the Indies,

[47] For examples, see Azara, 1923, 2:119-20; 1943, p. 170; Garay, 1942, p. 117.

which sent decrees in 1605 and 1606 to the Audiencia of Charcas, ordering that an inspector be sent to investigate the situation. Francisco de Alfaro was selected for the position, and he remained in the Province of Río de la Plata from 1610 to 1612. This inspection resulted in the publication of his famous ordinances which were designed to ameliorate the lot of the Indians in strict accordance with Crown policy. These ordinances were designed to abolish the illegal originario system of unpaid, year-round service, to reduce drastically the amount of labor of mitayo Indians, and to substitute paid labor under conditions regulated by public authority. The encomendero's privilege was limited to a fixed tribute, and his control was greatly reduced by allowing his Indians to contract to work for any Spaniard they wished. Religious instruction of the Indians was to be increased considerably, but, except for this, the tendency was to segregate and protect the Indians from contact with individual Spaniards and from control by them. Originario Indians were to have their own villages instead of living on the estates of the Spaniards, internal control of the pueblos was to be more fully in the hands of Indian officers, and Spaniards were prohibited from living in or even visiting the pueblos.

The application of these ordinances caused a great deal of confusion and elicited many protests. According to the lieutenant governor of Asunción, Sánchez Valderrama, the ordinances immediately resulted in disorder and ruin because many Indians, believing themselves free, forsook their work and failed to harvest the crops, and the Spaniards found themselves in misery.[48] A similar effect is described in Villarrica by the members of the town government, who argued that it was impossible to apply the ordinances.[49]

Many officials of towns in Argentina as well as in Paraguay protested vehemently to the King and the Council of the Indies,[50] and in 1618 the Council allowed some

[48] Sánchez Valderrama: 1612.

[49] ". . . tanta perturbacion ay en esta villa sobre las ordinanzas que en ella se an publicado que segun son tan regurosas e ymposibles de poderse cumplir ni guardar por la mucha pobreza y miseria que ay y se padesce en esta villa que si el senor oydor que las hizo la viera por visto de ojos por ventura hiziera otras que se pudieran mejor sobrellevar. . ." Gondra MS 1436.

[50] See the documents appended to Gandía, 1939.

important modifications of Alfaro's ordinances. It was provided that a Spanish administrator should live in the pueblos to teach the Indians to live "politically" and to "set the Indians a good example," and the tribute to be paid to the encomendero in products was changed from the equivalent of five pesos to six pesos per year. Personal service, which could be substituted for tribute should the Indians choose, was changed from thirty to sixty days a year. Some of the less important ordinances were also changed somewhat in favor of the encomendero.[51]

The ordinances of Alfaro, even with the modifications allowed by the Council of the Indies, were so inapplicable in Paraguay that they soon fell into discard. Even the originario system, which was Alfaro's main target, was not interrupted except for a short period of confusion.[52]

The disruption caused by Alfaro's ordinances was nearly coincident with two other important occurrences. The concern of Governor Hernandarias and the Spanish Crown over the lack of religious instruction of the Indians, and especially the failure of the Paraguayans to control the Indians of eastern Paraguay, who were strategically important as a buffer against the Brazilians, caused them to give the Jesuit order permission to colonize in this region. In 1609 the Jesuits founded their first missions in Guayrá, near the Paraná River, and from this date began the development of the famous system of thirty strictly controlled towns which contained about sixty thousand Guaraní. Until 1767, when the Jesuit order was expelled from the New World, the acculturation of these Indians was a separate process from that of Paraguay proper. The other important historical event following Alfaro's ordinances was the separation of the province of Río de la Plata into two parts in 1617. Buenos Aires became the capital of Río de la Plata, and Asunción the capital of Paraguay.

These developments had the effect of increasing the isolation and lack of trade with the outside world—two circumstances which had been important in rendering Alfaro's ordinances inapplicable in Paraguay. The Jesuits kept the Paraguayans from expanding successfully to the east and

[51] Consejo de Indias: 1618.

[52] Hernández, 1913, 2:114-15; Gandía, 1939, pp. 329-31; Azara, 1923, 2:126, and 1943, p. 168.

reduced the numbers of Indians available for exploitation by Paraguayan encomenderos. They were also able to compete successfully for the small amount of trade offered by Buenos Aires. The division of the province contributed to the importance of Buenos Aires, but correspondingly reduced the importance of Asunción. In Mitre's words: ". . . Paraguay, isolated, reduced to its own resources, deprived of the vivifying currents of immigration and the interchange of products, became stagnant and ceased to be the center of a fruitful and expanding civilization."[53]

The Spanish Crown had long since lost interest in the colony, for the region never produced any mineral wealth, nor did Paraguay produce any export commodity important to Spain. Purely geographic difficulties of access also limited intercourse with Europe, and, in addition, Paraguay was isolated because of artificial restrictions on trade. From 1535 to 1575 direct trade between Spain and the La Plata region was prohibited, and even after Buenos Aires was refounded in 1580, Peru and Panama retained their monopoly on South American trade and were able to persuade Spain to uphold it at the cost of the development of the port of Buenos Aires. According to Haring, "the La Plata region . . . was till near the end of the eighteenth century almost completely closed to the rest of the world."[54] This lack of contact with Europe and the near impossibility of overland trade with Peru reduced Paraguay to a subsistence economy with no recourse but self-sufficiency and small-scale barter trade between towns.

It is interesting to note how documents of all periods from the time of Irala to the end of the eighteenth century stress the general poverty and lack of money in Paraguay. It seems clear that this situation must have been the most direct and influential imperative which influenced the form of Spanish exploitation of the natives.

Irala's ordinances of 1541-47 indicate that all trade was exchange of produce within the colony and that there was a lack of any standard of value. Wages were paid in beans, corn, manioc, and so forth. At one time Irala tried to use knives as the standard of value.[55] López de

[53] Mitre, 1887, 1:19-20. This passage appears in English in Levene, 1937, p. 50.

[54] Haring, 1918, p. 40.

[55] Irala: 1541-47.

Velasco, in the period of 1571-74, made the following comment: " . . . they all have that which is necessary for sustenance, but no wealth in money, for there is none in the land: all their wealth is the agriculture of the country . . . . There are no commodities because there are no seaports; everyone puts what he wishes to exchange in the hands of a broker in a public house, placed by the city, and those who want to trade with others come there; because there is no money except some wedges or hatchets of iron. . . ."[56]

Ramírez de Velasco's ordinance 45, in 1597, states that "there is no gold or silver nor currency and the trade . . . is in wine, sugar, and other things . . . ."[57] Ruiz de Montoya, who was in Paraguay in the early 1600's, said of Asunción: " . . . they have no gold or silver mines, and there is no money whatever. Buying and selling is by the exchange of one thing for another . . . ."[58]

Sebastián de León, writing to the King in 1639, devoted his whole letter to recounting the extreme poverty of the Indians and the impossibility of extracting tribute from them because of the nature of the economy.[59] Del Techo, writing of Asunción of 1645, described quite fully the circumstances of the city, the inhabitants of which "know nothing of money, but live still by exchange of commodities, after the manner of antiquity . . . ."[60] Acarete du Biscay, another seventeenth-century visitor, said of the people of Asunción: " . . . having plenty of all things good to eat and drink, they give themselves up to Ease and Idleness, and don't much trouble themselves with Trading abroad, nor heaping up Money, which upon that account is very scarce among them . . . ."[61] Dobrizhoffer, who was in Paraguay in the middle of the eighteenth century, said:

[56]López de Velasco, 1894, pp. 551-52.

[57]Ramírez de Velasco: 1597.

[58]Ruiz de Montoya, 1892, pp. 16-17.

[59]" . . . no ha venido minerales como no los ay de plata ni trayendose de fuera no se alla en esta Ciudad ni corre otra cosa mas que los frutos que en ellos se recogen de las dhas labores asi los Indios pagan otros tributos ni aprovechamientos por que no ay de donde ni los ocupados en dhos oficios y por estar como estan en suma Pobreca huyen de ella . . ." Gondra MS 209a.

[60]Techo, 1744-46, p. 15.

[61]Acarete du Biscay, 1698, p. 11.

". . . money is used very rarely, if at all, its place being supplied by the exchange of commodities, as among the ancients . . . the want or ignorance of metals may be reckoned amongst the divine blessings and advantages of Paraguay."[62]

There were apparently very few inventions or native handicrafts of the Indians which could have been used for tribute. The commerce in yerba mate was steadily increasing in importance in Guayrâ, but it was a Spanish enterprise in which the natives functioned only as an unpaid labor force at the bidding of the Spaniards. There is no evidence that they ever marketed it themselves or submitted it as tribute payments.

The practical economic reasons which caused encomienda labor to be substituted for tribute brought the Spaniards and Indians into a symbiotic relationship with respect to subsistence activities and were, therefore, very important in promoting the mixing of the two cultures. The limited economy of Paraguay also had the effect of reducing the great gulf which has always existed between the philosophy and attitudes of Europeans and American Indians in economic matters. In other parts of Latin America the middle class ideals of the Spanish entrepreneurs as opposed to the native conception of production-for-use were, and often still are, an important factor inhibiting a mixture of the two cultures.[63] In Paraguay the circumstances never permitted the growth of a large class of traders and financiers whose interests and ideals would necessarily be opposed to the Indian viewpoint. The Spaniards in Paraguay were, truly enough, the exploiters, and the Indians were exploited, but as this occurred largely within a subsistence economy, it was a situation at least comprehensible to the Indians, and probably an even more acceptable one than it might have been under the conditions of a money economy.

The limited economy of Paraguay had influenced the exploitation of Guaraní labor from a very early date, as evidenced in Irala's first encomienda ordinances. As the encomienda system became further adjusted to the Paraguayan situation, it differed even more markedly from the classic encomienda of Spanish legal theory. The use of

[62]Dobrizhoffer, 1822, 1:216-18.

[63]Simpson, 1938b.

labor instead of tribute remained its most distinguishing characteristic, but, in addition, the Paraguayan encomienda differed from the "classic" encomienda in the means of control by the encomendero, amount of religious instruction, the prevalence of kin ties between Indians and encomenderos, and the position of mestizos in this relationship.

All of these features caused the acculturation of the Guaraní Indians to be more complete and more rapid than would have been the case under the formal encomienda envisaged by the Spanish Crown. As has been noted in the Introduction, the Crown's purpose was both to instruct and to protect the New World natives. After the disaster in the West Indies the increased anxiety to protect the Indians resulted in encomienda laws which tended to prevent their acculturation. In Paraguay the needs of the colonists in the unusual circumstances of their settlement caused them to ignore most of the Crown laws and adapt the encomienda system to the requirements of the local situation in ways which affected aboriginal culture. Specific and detailed evidence concerning the effect of this system on Guaraní acculturation is lacking, but many of the influences which must have resulted from the purely formal aspects of the encomienda system of control may be inferred.

II. THE EXPLORATORY PHASE: SPANISH-GUARANÍ RELATIONS FROM 1537 TO 1556

During the first twenty years of their residence in Asunción the Spaniards apparently regarded their stay as merely a temporary respite between the several arduous explorations. They needed food, labor, and military aid from their Guaraní allies, but were content to obtain these services by the most expeditious means and in such a way that the Guaraní remained willing collaborators. Thus, the Spaniards made no attempt at this time to institute the usual colonial methods of exploiting and controlling Indians in an encomienda system, which would have been alien to Guaraní custom. Instead of attempting to force the Indians to become adapted to the Spanish system, the Spanish soldiers expediently adjusted themselves to native habits by bringing Indian women to Asunción as wives and concubines and living by the contributions in food and services which their Indian relatives and allies freely provided.

This rather casual adaptation of the two peoples was typical of the exploratory period. In later times the encomienda system appeared and was a more characteristic Spanish institution, but the concubinage-kinship labor pattern was never entirely replaced, and it imparted its flavor to the whole history of Spanish-Guaraní acculturation in colonial Paraguay.

The character of these polygynous relations between the Spanish colonists and the Guaraní women[64] has often been considered one of the most notable aspects of the early colonial period of Paraguay. Rubio said: "One of the most interesting characteristics of the Spanish action in America was, as is known, the spontaneous fusion of the Spaniards with the indigenes. Paraguay constituted in this sense something truly extraordinary. . . . The intimate bonds of relationship which sprang up between Spaniards and Guaraní were the greatest guarantee of the alliance."[65]

Gandía has emphasized the importance of this situation in the following manner:

"The mixture of Spaniards and indigenes was realized in exemplary form in Paraguay. Domingo de Irala was the perfect colonizer who knew how to fuse an army of a few tens of Spaniards with a population of thousands and thousands of Indians. . . . Life in Asunción was compared to 'Mohammed's Paradise' because each Spaniard had a number of women which went from five and ten to a hundred. Among them were mothers, daughters, and sisters, and all of them customarily had marital relations with the conquistador who controlled them. The clerics cried to the heavens; but the Spaniards sealed familial alliances with the innumerable relatives of the Indian women and thus each of them could call himself an in-law, Tovaya, of hundreds of Indians. The Hispano-indigenous hearth of Paraguay, in this form, came to be constituted of several

[64]The term "polygyny" will be used hereafter to refer to these relations. The Spaniards regarded some of the women as legal wives, and others merely as concubines; to the Guaraní either case would have been considered customary marriage, thus from their point of view the use of the term seems justifiable.

[65]Rubio, 1942, p. 181.

thousands of Guaraní Indian men and women, and some few hundreds of Spanish soldiers. Peace was assured, and thanks to the immoralities of the Spaniards the colonization could be saved from the assaults of the Guaycurús and Payaguás."[66]

One of the features of the colonization of Paraguay which led to the intermarriage of Guaraní women and Spanish conquerors was the fact that the first expeditions were composed almost entirely of men. Gandía indicated that there were very few women with the Mendoza expedition and that some of them returned to Spain with Mendoza. He then presented documentary evidence which gave the names of four Spanish women who were in Asunción after Cabeza de Vaca's arrival in 1542.[67] A letter from Doña Isabel de Guevara in 1556 indicated that she was a member of the Mendoza expedition and referred to the presence of Spanish women, but did not mention the number.[68]

In 1552 the survivors of a new expedition to Paraguay, under Sanabria, arrived in Asunción. Sanabria had been given permission by the king to take eighty men with their families and twenty unmarried women, thus making a total of one hundred women.[69] This expedition spent five years en route. Lost ships, wrecks, trouble with the Indians, and captivity by the Portuguese in Brazil reduced their number so that only twelve men and seven women arrived in Asunción with Hernando de Salazar in 1552.[70]

Hernando de Trejo came later with a small group, but it is not known that there were any women with him. Thus, only twelve Spanish women have been noted through the first twenty years of settlement in Paraguay, although there may have been a few more.

In the absence of Spanish women affinal ties between Spaniards and Indians were established even before the initial settlement of Asunción. In the small Guaraní town of Tapuá Irala had taken an "india principal," and his soldiers followed his example. Some of them took as wives

[66]Gandía, 1939, pp. 33-34.

[67]Gandía, 1932b, pp. 120-24.

[68]I. Guevara: 1556.

[69]Royal cédula, cited by Gandía, 1932b, p. 131.

[70]According to his letter from Asunción, March 20, 1556, cited in Gandía, 1932b, p. 145.

the daughters of the important cacique, Moquirace.[71] Both Spanish and Guaraní leaders consciously encouraged these relationships as an aid in cementing the military alliance; the Guaraní chiefs gave their daughters to the Spaniards, and the Spaniards were urged to contract marriages with Guaraní women.

After the founding of Asunción this custom became even more significant in the alliance. For example, in 1539 a Guaraní uprising had been planned to take place during a great fiesta, but the Spaniards were warned of it by their Guaraní wives. Considering the value of Guaraní friendship, Irala merely imprisoned a few leaders and allowed everyone else to go unpunished. The Spaniards thus demonstrated their good intentions, and the Guaraní caciques reaffirmed their good faith by offering Irala and his captains their daughters and sisters to serve them, "assuming thereby to have dependence and affinity with them [the Spaniards], calling them 'cuñados' [in-law relatives], from whence the custom of calling the encomienda Indians by the name of Tobaya, which means cuñado . . . ."[72]

Guevara, in describing the building of Asunción by Irala, said: "The Guaraní friends aided in everything, [they were] so scrupulous in the observance of the capitulations, that they exceeded the terms of the obligations, and [they were] so obsequious in their relations with the Spaniards that they offered their daughters for service, and [the Spaniards] spent many years in scandalous concubinage with them."[73]

There are many documentary statements as to the numbers of Guaraní women who lived as wives and concubines of the Spaniards, but, as might be expected, major discrepancies are evident in the testimony. Irala wrote that prior to the abandonment of Buenos Aires in 1541 there were seven hundred Guaraní women serving the Spaniards in Asunción.[74] At this time the garrison of Asunción was composed of 250 to three hundred Spaniards. This makes an average of fewer than three women per Spaniard. As this was only four years after the founding of Asunción, it

[71]Moreno, 1926, p. 33.

[72]Díaz de Guzmán, 1943, p. 110.

[73]J. Guevara, 1836, p. 96.

[74]Quoted in Moreno, 1926, p. 25.

may be that the Spaniards had not yet completely adopted the concubinage pattern of later years. In subsequent years many Spaniards described tremendous "harems" in Asunción. Francisco Gonzales Paniagua wrote to the King in 1545 that some Spaniards had seventy wives, and that "one is poor who has only five or six, most having 15, 20, 30 and 40." Alonso Angulo, writing in the same year, said virtually the same thing.[75] Gerónimo Ochoa de Eizaguirre also wrote to the King in 1545 of "the great shamelessness of the Spaniards," who each had twenty Indian women,[76] and Martín Gonzales, writing in 1556, said that some Christians had eighty to one hundred women.[77]

These figures are undoubtedly exaggerations. It is apparent from the context of the letters that the writers were scandalized by the immorality and were anxious to impress the King with the enormity of the crime. The cleric, Martín Gonzales, in particular, was a great opponent of Irala. Further evidence of his anxiety to discredit the regime will be noted.

The sixteenth-century Spanish chronicler, Antonio de Herrera, writing of the period of Irala's governorship between 1545 and 1556, said that the Spanish residents of Paraguay had three thousand mestizo sons[78]—thus, six thousand children. The greatest number of Spaniards had been six hundred in 1542, which makes an average of ten children for each Spaniard. It would seem that an average of about three women for one Spaniard might have borne that number of children.

By 1556 the numbers of Spaniards had diminished considerably. Irala related that when he established the encomiendas at that time, he divided twenty thousand Indians among 320 or more Spaniards.[79] If perhaps two thousand of these Indians were of an age and circumstance which qualified them to be wives or concubines of the Spaniards, only seven women were available to each Spaniard—in addition, of course, to any women he already may have had.

[75] These two letters are quoted in Gandía, 1932b, p. 21.

[76] Ibid., p. 128

[77] Gonzales: 156, p. 609.

[78] Herrera, 1934, 1:184.

[79] Irala: 1556b, p. 544.

It seems clear that the testimony attributing an average of twenty wives or more to each Spaniard is not accurate. There is, of course, always a possibility that a few men may have had that many, whereas others had no more than one or two. The Spaniards were not all of equal rank, and the majority of those called "conquistadores" were no more than foot soldiers. It is known that the encomiendas of Indians were divided according to the "merits" of the Spaniards. Probably, the descriptions of the "harems" of twenty or more women was a complaint against only a few Spaniards of high rank.[80]

During the early phase of the settlement of Asunción these polygynous households of the Spaniards had an interesting connection with the use of Indian labor and with the general integration of Spaniards into a Guaraní culture pattern. The Guaraní wives and concubines were important to the Spaniards not only for sexual reasons and for furthering the alliance between the two peoples, as has been discussed, but also as sources of labor. These women were often considered servants as well as wives, and their work, in addition to household chores, was also concerned with food production. From the Guaraní point of view, the Spaniards appear to have been regarded as chiefs, probably because of their military prowess, so that a Spaniard was expected to have several Guaraní wives, the number depending somewhat on his status. His connection with a Guaraní lineage as an in-law and chief entitled him to security, gifts of agricultural produce, and labor services from the whole group.

Moreno said that the women were given to the conquistadores "as companions in the home and as agents of production, for it was they who worked the fields." [81] The cleric, Francisco de Andrada, in a letter of March 1, 1545, wrote: "We find, Señor, in this land a very bad custom: that it is the women who sow and reap the crop."[82] One of the settlers of Asunción, Diego Téllez de Escobar,

[80] Irala himself had at least seven Indian wives. His testament provided for the inheritance of their children, and specifically named the women. He may also have had additional women who were childless, or whose children he did not regard as legitimate heirs. Irala: 1556c, pp. 560-61.

[81] Moreno, 1926, pp. 24-25.

[82] Quoted in Gandía, 1932b, pp. 18-19.

reported to the King that it was "the custom of the land that the women work and produce the food in the fields. . . ."[83] The anonymous Relación del Río de la Plata of 1545, in discussing a trip upriver from Asunción and trouble with the Payaguás there, related that it was necessary to come downriver to get food from "the Cario [Guaraní] who are our friends from whom we have a very great service, as much from them as their women who provide us with food."[84] As Téllez de Escobar described the situation: "It was the custom of the Indians of the land to serve the Christians and give them their daughters or sisters and to come to their houses in a spirit of kinship and friendship. The Christians were thus served because they had many children by the natives, and for this reason the Indians came to aid them as to the home of kinsmen. . . ."[85] Irala himself briefly described the Guaraní in 1553, as "people without lord [señor] nor leader whom they obey, nor do they pay tribute to the conquistadores, but only give personal service and because of ancient custom . . . all the Indians, or the greater part of them, are indebted to all the conquerors because of having given their daughters, sisters, and relatives whom they serve in everything. . . ."[86]

The cleric Gonzales Paniagua in a letter of March 3, 1545, was scandalized because the Spaniards used to refer to the Indians who served them as "relatives" or "in-laws" instead of servants.[87]

It is said that in modern Paraguay the women still do much of the productive work of the country. Travelers and writers and even some historians relate this to the various wars--especially the War of the Triple Alliance in the 1870's--which caused such a notable scarcity of men.[88] The passages quoted above would seem to indicate, however, that the important economic role of women may well

[83] " . . . la costumbre de aquellatierra es que las mugeres travajan y hazen las comydas en el campo." Gondra MS 725ℓ.

[84] Relación del Río de la Plata, p. 44.

[85] Téllez de Escobar: n.d., p. 270.

[86] Dorantes: 1553, p. 486.

[87] Quoted in Gandía, 1932b, p. 20.

[88] For examples, see Kirkpatrick, 1939, p. 174; and Gunther, 1941, p. 272.

have its roots in the culture of the aborigines, as a trait which existed before the Spaniards ever set foot in Paraguay.

There may have been a tendency for the Spaniards, or some of them at least, to take advantage of their power over the women and their relatives and to treat them somewhat ruthlessly. The aforementioned cleric, Gonzales Paniagua, in a letter of February 18, 1545,[89] complained that the Carios had been mistreated since Cabeza de Vaca's imprisonment and were in the same condition as slaves. It is evident from the context of this letter, which was written in protest of Irala's imprisonment of Cabeza de Vaca, that the cleric was anxious to discredit Irala; consequently, it is probably not just to accept this information completely. Diego Téllez de Escobar reported that Irala actually gave permission to the Spaniards "to go to the houses and villages of the Indians and take from them their women and daughters."[90]

Fray Bernardo de Armenta, in a letter of October 10, 1544, accused the Spaniards of selling the women to one another.[91] Gandía cited several similar accusations made at that time, but noted that clerics or men opposed to polygyny were responsible for all of them; accordingly, he discounted their testimony.[92]

Doubtless, certain Spaniards were often cruel. It is nevertheless true that personal service persisted without any particular disturbances and became so firmly implanted that it continued to be one of the important characteristics of Spanish-Guaraní relations throughout most of the colonial period. Had the situation been too disagreeable to the Guaraní, it would seem that the small garrison of Spaniards might have been easily overthrown. The fact is that the situation was precarious for the Spaniards, and they knew it. It seems reasonable to assume, therefore, that the

[89]Quoted in Gandía, 1932b p. 76.

[90]"Ubo entre los cristianos muchas diferencias y dio domyngo de Yrala licencia a muchas personas para que fuesen a tierra y casa de los yndios a tomarles sus mugeres e hijas e otros muchos y muy grandes agravios por tener a aquellas personas de su mano para poder hazer lo que quisiese en la tierra." Gondra MS 725ℓ. Tellez' manuscript is also a diatribe against Irala.

[91]Gandía, 1932b, pp. 81-83.

[92]*Ibid.*

Spaniards were influenced to be more cautious than they might otherwise have been.

Several ordinances of Cabeza de Vaca and of Irala prior to 1556 indicate that the leaders, at least, were conscious of the need for careful treatment of their Guaraní allies and providers. Cabeza de Vaca, for example, in his ordinances, forbade that "anyone should bargain for or contract Indian women with others [Spaniards], without permission of his lordship [the governor], because they are free . . ." and instructed "that the Indian women of the Christians be allowed to go to their houses where their parents and relatives live to see and visit them without any difficulty. . . ."[93] In the same group of ordinances he prohibited any Spaniard from going to the Indians' houses without permission from the governor. The governor also was aware of the fact that interpreters, by reason of their semiofficial position and ability to speak both Spanish and Guaraní, were in a more favorable position than others to cheat the Indians. He, therefore, ordered that the interpreters sent to the houses or localities of the Indians were to contract that for which they were sent and were not to intervene directly or indirectly in other affairs. The Indians could not be ill-treated by word or in any other manner, under penalty of eight days in jail and a fine of one thousand maravedis, nor were the interpreters allowed to use an Indian relative or servant to contract for them with the other Indians. After visiting Indians on some legitimate business, they were to report immediately to the governor everything that they had done.[94]

Alvar Núñez Cabeza de Vaca's term as governor was broken by his imprisonment in 1544. Irala then became the leading figure until his death in 1556 or 1557. It seems likely that, coincident with the evident discord among the Spaniards caused by Irala's seizure of power, the rules for conduct of Spaniards toward the Guaraní must have been relaxed because Irala was bidding for popular Spanish support. Rubio felt that it was lack of discipline after Cabeza de Vaca was removed from the scene which

[93]Cabeza de Vaca: 1542.

[94]Ibid.

led to the short-lived Guaraní insurrection of 1545.[95] There is evidence that Irala was aware of the possibility of difficulties with the Indians at about that time, for some of his first ordinances required that the Spaniards should be armed when going into the country. Further, he had ordered that for a space of two months no one should force any Indian man to work, although the Indians could present themselves for work according to their own desires. He also ordered that no Spaniard should enter the Indians' homes.[96] In his ordinances of 1547 Irala repeated that it was forbidden to go to the Indian houses or within fifty paces of them in search of missing Indians or to look for anything, or to buy anything, without express permission of the lieutenant governor.[97]

The foregoing data imply a necessity, probably for security reasons, of restricting the control of the Guaraní by Spaniards. This held at least during the early period of colonization, when the Spaniards were too few to risk imposing their will by sheer force. As has been seen, when the Spaniards did get out-of-hand shortly after Irala's succession to the governorship, some of the Indians responded violently in a brief uprising. This short period of tension excepted, the amount of control and of service achieved by means of the system of servitude that had developed must have been adequate. No changes were introduced until 1556, when the Indians were placed in encomiendas, which had been finally granted because of pressure from Spain rather than owing to any exigency in the situation in Paraguay.

The account that has been given so far of Spanish-Indian relations indicates that the situation around Asunción was very favorable for rapid acculturation of both Spaniards and Indians. The most obvious circumstance is the presence of Guaraní women in the Spanish households. In the absence of Spanish women Guaraní household customs, cookery, child training, and so forth, probably prevailed to a considerable extent. On the other hand, the agricultural labors of the Guaraní women must have been directly

[95]Rubio, 1942, pp. 220-21.

[96]Irala: 1541-47, pp. 429-32.

[97]*Ibid.*, p. 433.

under the Spaniards' supervision, so that some European tools and techniques were available to the Indians, as well as a few new crops. The Spaniards, too, because of the failure of relief ships to arrive from Europe, must have learned quickly to adapt their tastes to the Guaraní staples, manioc and maize, and to the several tropical fruits and minor crops. Since documentary evidence of the particulars of daily life is scanty for this early period, it is impossible to recount in detail the exchange of specific cultural elements. It seems clear, however, that the early years of hardship and isolation must have made the Spaniards quite dependent on the subsistence offered by the Guaraní and must have somewhat limited the amount of European crops and tools they could provide the Indian women and their relatives.

The Indians who lived outside this orbit of personal service and relationship which was centered at Asunción were not, of course, so immediately affected. Before 1556 the Spaniards made little or no attempt to control or exploit the Guaraní who lived in outlying areas. Great numbers of Guaraní men were used as auxiliaries on Spanish expeditions, but except for this association there is no evidence of much Spanish contact. One might surmise that there was probably trade and that, despite the failure of supply ships from Europe, some European goods must have reached the Indians. Metal tools are usually among the first European elements to become dispersed widely by trade among aborigines. In Paraguay, however, there was no iron ore, and, as little relief was available from Europe, metal tools were notably scarce. Axes, wedges, and knives became so highly prized in Asunción that they were used as standards of value.[98] Other elements of cultural importance, such as European domestic animals, firearms, wheeled vehicles, boats, new crops, and agricultural techniques, did not become important in outlying districts until 1556, when the Indians were placed in encomiendas.

III. THE TRANSITIONAL PHASE

The transition from the temporary settlement of the exploratory phase to the direct and purposeful acculturation

[98]Zavala, 1946.

of the Indians which occurred after the Spaniards resolved to colonize the country permanently was initiated by the 1556 grants of encomiendas. This meant that the Indians were to become more strictly and formally controlled and that their lives would be changed in accordance with patterns implicit in the institution of the encomienda. Asunción was now to become a true colonial society with its economy based on exploitation of local Indians. All wealth, status, and security to be gained by the Spaniards were now seen to depend on their control of the Indians rather than on any fortuitous discoveries of mineral wealth.

This attitude not only caused the Spaniards to become more systematic in their control and exploitation of the Indians in the vicinity of Asunción, but eventually resulted in a wider extension of the encomienda to include the Guaraní of more distant areas. The need to extend colonization was aggravated by two conditions. The Indian population was being reduced by European diseases and possibly also by the retreat of some Indians from the areas of Spanish domination. Coincident with this diminution in Indian population was the rapid increase in the numbers of mestizo sons of the original Spaniards. Proud and ambitious men, they were instrumental in founding new colonial towns in eastern Paraguay and in Argentina, for Asunción no longer offered them the possibility of becoming encomenderos of large numbers of Indians. Eventually, Asunción itself was dominated by mestizos as the peninsular Spaniards died out.

The encomienda system, once it was firmly established and extended, had important cultural consequences for the Guaraní Indians. New tools, crops, and techniques were introduced, social systems were changed, numbers and distribution of the population were altered. The lack of a cash crop, isolation, demographic factors, and the influence of Guaraní culture were also to alter the nature of the encomienda system and the culture of the "Spanish" encomenderos. Most of these changes did not occur simultaneously with the first appearance of the encomienda system, but were results of a slow process of adaptation to local conditions. The changing character of Spanish-Guaraní relations in the transitional phase of the colonization had certain immediate and obvious effects, but the firmly seated and more pervasive cultural changes which developed subsequently are discussed in Chapters IV and V.

Irala's Grants of Encomiendas in 1556

In 1553 the factor, Pedro Dorantes, in conjunction with two other royal officers wrote an official demand (requerimiento) to Irala that a system of forming encomiendas and new towns be instituted in accordance with the desires of the King.[99] Irala was disposed to follow the order, and in 1556 the Indians in the vicinity of Asunción were divided among the Spaniards, and the following ordinances were presented "for the good and advantageous indoctrination and conservation and good treatment of the said Indians. . . .

1. The encomended Indians are obliged to obey their chiefs and mayors, and must live permanently in their houses and villages, and not leave them for other villages and houses. Nor may they allow Indians from other encomiendas to reside in their village.

2. The encomended Indians may not trade or contract with any other person except their encomendero. Nor may they give or contract their women, daughters, sisters, or female relatives to any Spaniard, in order to avoid passions and disagreements.

3. The encomendero may not ask, procure, or contract with his Indians for Indian women.

4. The Indians must not be given an excessive amount of work, and the Indians cannot be lent for work to any other person without the express wish of the said Indians . . . .

5. The said Indians are obliged to serve their encomenderos in building houses, labor, repairs and agricultural work, hunting and fishing, and any other enterprises --and they must obey and accomplish that which they are ordered. The encomenderos may not have buildings made or fields cleared in order to sell, but only for their own use. . . .

6. The encomendero must treat his Indians very well and favor them and aid them in every possible way and not give

[99] Dorantes: 1553.

them excessive work, and [he must] instruct and indoctrinate them in our sacred Catholic faith.

7. No one may be served at one time by more than a fourth part of the number of Indians in his encomienda.

8. No one may send Indians or servants to the lands and towns of Indians to contract anything, except to those of their encomienda.

9. An encomendero visiting his Indians may not ask for or take anything from the home of the Indians. The Indians are obliged only to give him food for two or three days. They are not obliged to give him chicken or pork, but only the ordinary food, unless they freely want to for moderate payment.

10. The Indians are obliged to give the traveler porters and guides to the next village.

11, 12. [These ordinances are not pertinent.]

13. The encomenderos should have in their houses two or three boys of 10 years or under from their encomiendas that they may learn the Christian doctrine and how to live properly, because at 12 or 13 years of age they can return to their homes and instruct their families.

14. No one may interfere with the Indians' lands, pastures, hunting, or fishing rights, or village land which they possess by custom.

15. On the death of an Indian, the female survivors must remain in the same encomienda, and same house, as opposed to the ancient custom of returning to their original homes.

16. Indians, chiefs or not, who come to complain justly of being mistreated or of too much work should be heard in justice and be maintained and guarded.

17. Every year, after the said Indians are in an encomienda, inspectors (visitadores) shall go over the land with a notary and interpreter, to obtain information of any crimes. The inspectors should be honorable and conscientious and see that the present ordinances are executed with all rigor.

18. Should any Indians rebel or not wish to serve and contribute to the encomendero, the other men who have encomiendas shall contribute their services and arms to the pacification of the rebellious Indians."[100]

[100]Irala: 1556a. These are paraphrased condensations of the original ordinances. Every effort was made to preserve the exact meaning.

It is difficult to judge the accuracy of these ordinances as a source of information on the specific details of cultural change which the Indians were to undergo. Since they were a result of prompting from the King of Spain and his royal officers, it is inevitable that many of the ordinances should reflect Crown policy, whether or not there was any likelihood that they would be enforced in Paraguay.

The somewhat idealized form of the encomienda which is revealed in these first ordinances had a specifically local character in one respect. Ordinances 5 and 7 require labor and personal service of the Indians, and there is no word about tribute. As Irala had stated in his Relación Breve: "They have no means to be of service except with their persons."[101] This is in direct contradiction to contemporary Crown laws which were supposed to apply to all of Spanish America. These laws had abolished encomienda labor and substituted the payment of tribute in its place, and after 1549 they had radically changed the character of encomiendas in Mexico and Peru.[102] In spite of the Crown's continued prohibition, encomienda labor persisted as characteristic of Paraguay throughout the colonial period and is probably one of the important reasons why Spanish-Guaraní acculturation was different from that in other regions of the New World. The subsequent cultural effect of this feature of the Paraguayan encomienda is discussed in a later chapter. It may be noted at this point, however, that the imperatives of the Paraguayan economy were already reflected even in the legalistic form of the inchoate encomienda. Within the framework of what was essentially a subsistence economy tribute was seen to be an unworkable form of exploitation.

Most of the remaining ordinances are more or less typical of the Crown's usual policy. Ordinances 1 and 14 state that the encomendero did not have rights to the land

[101]Irala: 1556b, p. 544.

[102]Zavala, 1943, pp. 85-86. E. Cardozo suggested that the "New Laws" were not enforced in Paraguay because of isolation and difficulties of communication. He then cited a document from the cleric, Martín Gonzales (1558), who asked Governor Vergara to apply the 1542 laws. Ortiz de Vergara replied that he did not know of them legally, and that he considered them totally inapplicable to Paraguay. E. Cardozo, 1938, pp. 126-27.

of his Indians, that he should not interfere with its use, and that the Indians were to remain permanently in their own villages. Neither of these ordinances was peculiar to Paraguay, for in no part of the New World did the encomendero have legal rights to his Indians' land,[103] nor did the Indians have freedom of movement, but in Paraguay their application had an effect that was not anticipated by those who originally created the laws. These general rules grew out of the problems the Crown faced in its attempts to protect the Indians of Mexico and Peru. In these regions of comparatively dense aboriginal population and large permanent towns, the greatest disruptive effect occurred whenever the scarce and valuable Indian lands were encroached on by Spaniards and when the Indians were dislodged from their towns. The application of the laws thus tended to prevent the acculturation of the Indians. In Paraguay, however, since there was plenty of arable land, especially under the more intensive agricultural techniques of the Europeans, it was not necessary to dislocate the Indian villages by progressive encroachment on their land. On the contrary, the aboriginal Guaraní practiced a shifting agriculture which involved periodic relocation of their villages; consequently, the Spaniards must have intervened in the aboriginal techniques of land utilization, since they enforced stability of Guaraní villages. Thus, ordinances which helped to preserve aboriginal village and land systems in Mexico and Peru had the effect of altering them in Paraguay. These ordinances were undoubtedly enforced in Paraguay, as the encomendero found it necessary for Indians to live in a permanent village.

Ordinance 15 specifically changed one aboriginal custom by providing that on the death of the Indian husband his wife, or wives (and children, of course), must continue to occupy the house of the deceased, instead of returning home to her consanguineal family, "as was the ancient custom." Like the previous ordinance regarding permanency, this was probably enforced, as the encomendero would be loath to lose any of his Indians. An important change in Indian social organization is thus implied. In virtually all primitive societies the unilateral

[103]Kirkpatrick, 1942; Zavala, 1943, p. 83.

consanguineal family is the stable unit through which property is inherited and in which the security of individuals is provided through mutual aid; the conjugal relationship of men and women of different blood lines is much less stable and is relatively nonfunctional in the inheritance of property.[104] Ordinance 15 served to force marital property to be retained by the surviving wife, thus stabilizing the conjugal family after the European pattern. One might also expect that the Spaniards would have discouraged the aboriginal tendency toward easy "divorce" or separation of married Indians, both for ideological reasons stemming from Christianity and for the practical purpose of maintaining permanency of residence among the encomienda Indians.

Ordinances 6 and 13 indicate that one of the intentions of the encomienda system was to teach the Catholic faith to the Indians, even though there were never enough clerics in Paraguay. The rather ridiculous provision of ordinance 13 that two or three boys under ten years of age should be taught the faith in order to teach their own parents implies that in 1556 Irala was concerned with the same problem of implanting Catholicism that was to be a continuing worry of the governors for the rest of the century.

The remainder of Irala's ordinances do not differ from the usual encomienda rules which were current in the New World. They pay a sort of lip service to the humanitarian concerns of the Spanish Crown, but they can be ignored as sources of information on the actual state of affairs, for, as later developments show, there was a great gulf between the law and the deed in Paraguay.

Certain more explicit characteristics of these first encomiendas are revealed in documents from this period. Antonio de la Trinidad wrote in 1556 that the Indians are "greatly aided by being in encomiendas because they are a very poor people and they are given tools to make their houses and till their fields and cut wood, and they are taught the doctrine, and some are dressed in cotton, and it is not allowed that anyone do them injury nor take anything from them as was done in previous times."[105]

[104] Benedict, 1936.

[105] Trinidad: 1556, p. 227.

There were many objections to the way Irala apportioned the Indians, especially because of the small number in each encomienda. Irala had said he divided perhaps twenty thousand Indians among 320 "or more" Spaniards.[106] This is only sixty-two or sixty-three Indians per Spaniard if they were divided equally. According to Juãn de Salazar in a letter to the Council of the Indies, the Indians in the encomiendas were so few in number that, because of the "poverty of the country, the Christians cannot sustain themselves in it." The thousands of Indians he himself was supposed to get in return for his services and expenses were not even two hundred. He then asked the Council that his encomienda be given in perpetuity as he had no wealth to leave to his wife and children.[107]

Juãn Salmerón, writing to the King in 1556, also complained of the small size of the encomiendas and asked that the number of encomenderos be reduced to one hundred; thus each encomienda would be enlarged and the Indians would be saved from so much work.[108] He further suggested that each encomienda have at least three hundred Indians so that these would be better treated and the Spaniards better provided for: ". . . and this is very little with respect to the Repartimientos that can be given in . . . Peru and the Province of the Xaraies where they can give as a repartimiento four and five thousand Indians. . . ." Salmerón, like Salazar, asked that the encomiendas be given in perpetuity.[109]

Irala's ordinances made no specific provision for the inheritance of the encomiendas, but it is indicated in the foregoing statements of Salmerón and Salazar that they were not granted in perpetuity. Irala had also requested that permanent rights to the Indians be granted,[110] thus demonstrating that he was not free to make this provision. Salmerón's request of the Council of the Indies that he be allowed to leave his encomienda to his wife and children

[106]Irala: 1556b, p. 544.

[107]Salazar: 1556, pp. 579-82.

[108]There were exactly one hundred conquistadores remaining from the original Mendoza expedition, according to Antonio de la Trinidad: 1556, p. 228.

[109]Salmerón: n.d., pp. 235-36.

[110]Irala: 1556b, p. 544.

indicates that the encomiendas may have been granted for the lifetime of only the original encomendero.[111]

It is difficult to deduce from the documents of this period just what effect the new encomiendas had on the previously discussed system of household and agricultural service based on polygynous marriages. Diego Téllez de Escobar complained of the injury done to the Spaniards by the encomienda laws "because the Indians do not come to serve as they used to."[112] This may possibly mean that the services of the relatives of a Spaniard's wives were suspended because some of them would be, inevitably, members of another man's encomienda and could not therefore undertake services for any one other than their own encomendero. Also, the fact that only one-fourth of the number of Indians in an encomienda could be used at any one time may have been a restriction which was partly responsible for Téllez' complaint. There is no evidence that the system of household, year-round service by the Indian women was actually abolished, although Irala's ordinances may have been intended to do away with it, or at least to give such an appearance. The time of Irala's grants was perhaps a period of flux and uncertainty, or the household service may have remained relatively secure except for the diminution of service by the women's relatives alluded to by Téllez. However this may be, there is plenty of evidence that the Indians who served the year around continued to do so during most of the period under consideration, and until much later times. This kind of service became institutionalized as the originario type of encomienda (see Chapter IV). If Irala abolished it in accordance with Dorantes' requerimiento, it was only for a short time.

The objections raised to the large number of encomiendas and the resulting scarcity of Indians in any one

[111]Azara said that Irala decreed that the encomienda should belong to two generations, and that following that period the Indians should enjoy complete liberty, as the Spaniards did, paying only a tribute to the treasury, 1923, 2:118. Azara did not disclose the source of this information. It is possible that he judged this from the fact that the Crown favored the principle of freedom for the encomienda after the period of the original encomendero and one heir. See, Solórzano, Pereira, 1930, 2:191.

An "Informe" to the King from the Marqués de Aviles, in 1800, likewise related that Irala gave encomiendas which could be inherited by the second generation only. Aviles: 1800, p. 28.

[112]Tellez de Escobar: n.d., p. 270.

encomienda are obviously caused by the fact that some of the original Spaniards who had been prominent in the conquest were not favored sufficiently in the apportionment of Indians. Men who arrived later with Cabeza de Vaca, and thus were considered less deserving, had received them too. This caused the number of encomenderos to be too large.[113]

These complaints against Irala's decrees are important, for they reveal two definite facts. In the first place, the context of the complaints indicates that the previous hopes entertained by the Spaniards of finding undiscovered mineral wealth were at an end and that Asunción was now considered a permanent settlement, with the interest of the settlers centered on control of Indians as a basis of life. The instructions from the King to Irala in 1555, which ordered the establishment of encomiendas, also required him to cease his attempts at discovery and conquest and to devote himself to the colony already established.[114] The second fact of importance is related to the Spaniards' dissatisfaction with the numbers of natives allotted to them. The desire for more Indians in encomienda served to stimulate the establishment of new settlements in areas where more Indians were available.

The Founding of New Towns

The first attempts to extend the Spanish colonization to areas outside the immediate region of Asunción were in Guayrá in the Alto Paraná River basin, which is now partly in eastern Paraguay and partly in Brazil and Argentina. This development was a result of the ambitions of Paraguayan colonists who wished to control additional Indians and was also a response to a Crown order. The Spanish Crown was concerned above all with consolidating as large an area as possible and defending it against the aggressions of the Portuguese colonists of Brazil.[115]

[113]This is supported by an interpretation by Díaz de Guzmán, 1943, p. 200.

[114]Rubio, 1942, pp. 263-64.

[115]The so-called Mamelucos or Paulistas were already raiding the Guaraní who lived in Guayrá. Díaz de Guzmán, 1943, pp. 183-84.

Irala had already made an expedition to this region in 1553 in response to requests for aid from the Guaraní chiefs of the area. In 1554, following this expedition, he also had sent a group of sixty Spaniards under Rodríquez de Vergara to found the village called Ontiveros, expressly for the purpose of keeping the region secured.[116]

Díaz de Guzmán related that the sixty soldiers who had founded Ontiveros encountered a "great number of natives there," and "were well received by them."[117] One cacique in particular, a Guaraní named Canendiyú, had a village nearby and "was a very good friend of the Spaniards. . . .[118] At this time the natives of that province were very peaceful and quiet, and such was their devotion and obedience, that no matter what arduous task was ordered by the General, it was promptly executed."[119] As this town was founded before the system of encomiendas was begun in Paraguay, it can be assumed that a method of unlimited personal service was instituted.

In 1557 Irala sent Ruí Díaz de Melgarejo to found a new settlement in Guayrá with one hundred Spaniards who had been discontented with the state of affairs in Asunción. With these and the remainder of the small garrison of Ontiveros, which was now abandoned, he founded Ciudad Real near the Paraná, three leagues north of the former site of Ontiveros. In this region, according to the mestizo chronicler, Díaz de Guzmán: ". . . the Spaniards found forty thousand 'fuegos' of Indians, each 'fuego' being understood as one Indian with his wife and children, although it was always much more. These were given in encomienda to seventy residents, who for some years had them very peacefully, the encomenderos being treated with great respect by the natives, and being very well supplied with products of the soil such as wine, sugar, cotton, cloth, and wax; their looms had the best reputation of all in the state."[120]

An expedition toward the west was begun in 1558 by Nufro de Chávez with 150 Spaniards and fifteen hundred

[116]Rubio, 1942, p. 263; Díaz de Guzmán, 1943, pp. 183-84.

[117]Díaz de Guzmán, 1943, p. 184.

[118]Ibid.

[119]Ibid., pp. 186-87.

[120]Ibid., pp. 206-8.

Indians. They founded the short-lived Nueva Asunción in 1559, and in 1561 the city of Santa Cruz de la Sierra in eastern Bolivia.[121] The next town to be founded was Santa Fé in 1573, by Juán de Garay, who also re-established Buenos Aires in 1580. Inasmuch as these three towns were not in Paraguay, they will receive no further attention.

Villa Rica del Espiritú Santo, in the Province of Guayrá, was founded in 1576, but the original site was soon abandoned, and the people, including their encomiendas of Indians, changed their location several times.[122] In 1588 Alonso de Vera founded San Juán de Vera de las Siete Corrientes (now Corrientes), and, at the same time, three towns of Indian encomiendas, Ohomá, Itatí, and Santa Lucía. Several other Spanish towns were formed in various places during this period, but they did not long survive.

One significant new aspect of this period in Paraguay was the increasingly important role of mestizos in furthering the settlement of new towns. The great increase in numbers of mestizos and their relatively high social and legal status have already been mentioned. These new "Spaniards" were of tremendous importance in giving vigor to the new phase of the colonial period in Paraguay. For example, in the founding of Santa Fé, Juán de Garay was accompanied by "nine Spaniards and seventy-five young men who were natives of this land," and of the seventy-three men who resettled Buenos Aires, "ten were Spaniards and the others were natives of the country."[123]

Another important aim of the policy of expanding colonization was control of Indians by founding Indian towns. Azara has briefly described this policy in the following words:

"Inasmuch as they constantly received orders and exhortations to extend the explorations and conquests, without having funds and necessary means, Domingo Martínez de Irala, who regulated everything related to the conquest of the country, invented a way of making progress without expense. If he knew that some place there were savages

[121]Rubio, 1942, pp. 292-97.

[122]R. I. Cardozo, 1938a, p. 128.

[123]Levene, 1937, pp. 41-42.

who were few in number, he gave possession, as encomendero, to whomever would undertake, at his own expense, to bring these savages together with another village of Indians who were already 'reduced,' or to form a new village if he wished. Then, if he who was given this encomienda could not 'reduce' them . . . a small troop of soldiers would unite to force the Indians to be established in a town, and he would hold them as an 'encomienda de Mitayos.' But if the chief suspected that the Indians were very numerous (as happened in the Provinces of Guayrá and Chiquitos and in the country of Jérez), he would have them reconnoitered, and then being certain, he would send a company of Spaniards to found a fair-sized town. These Spaniards would divide the Indians and form encomiendas, sometimes of originarios, sometimes of yanaconas,[124] sometimes of mitayos, according to the circumstances we have previously explained."[125]

The foundation of permanent villages of Indians was a policy dating from 1538, when eleven pueblos were formed.[126] No others were organized until the activity in Guayrá in 1555, to which reference has been made. In that one year thirteen more encomienda towns were founded: Loreto, San Ignacio-Miri, San Xavier, San José, Anunciación, San Miguel, San Antonio, San Pedro, Santo Tomé, Angeles, Concepción, San Pablo, and Jesús María. After the Spanish settlement of Villa Rica, fourteen more Indian villages were formed in that region between 1579 and 1610: Perico-Guazú, Jesuí, Curumiay, Pacurú, Ohomá, Guacarás, Baradero, Itatý, Santa Lucía, Tarey, Bomboy, Caaguazú, Caazapá, Yutý.[127]

The two Spanish settlements in Eastern Paraguay, Villarrica and Ciudad Real, and the twenty-seven encomienda towns of Indians which served them underwent a great many vicissitudes and hardships after their founding. These

[124] This usage is unusual. Ordinarily "yanacona" is used synonymously with "originario."

[125] Azara, 1923, 2:118.

[126] Azara said that two others, Itá and Yaguarón, had been founded in 1536. The eleven founded in 1538 were Areguá, Altos, Yoís, Tobatý, Ipané, Guarambaré, Atirá, Maracayú, Terecaný, Ibiraparyá, Candelaria. Azara, 1923, 2:129.

[127] *Ibid.*

Spaniards and the Indians they controlled acted as a buffer against the raids of the Paulistas. As a consequence, they had a difficult time; the Spaniards were few and were not reinforced from Asunción, and they never succeeded in acculturating the bulk of the large Indian population of the region. As a result of their failure and the increasing danger from Brazil, the Jesuits finally were sent in to complete the colonization.

The Role of Mestizos

As the peninsular Spaniards grew older and fewer in numbers during the latter half of the sixteenth century, the mestizos began to assume the position and role previously occupied by the original conquistadores. The historical change from the exploratory period to the phase of permanent settlement was roughly coincident with a gradual shift in the relative proportions of the pure Spanish, mestizo, and Indian elements making up the population.

The number of peninsular Spaniards in Paraguay was greatest after Cabeza de Vaca's arrival in 1542. There were at that time about six hundred men, most of them still young enough to continue vigorously the various explorations in search of gold and silver in the hope of returning eventually to Spain as wealthy men. The hardships of the expeditions and casualties from wars with hostile tribes caused a gradual reduction in their numbers, and as time went on old age also took its toll. In 1556 Jaime Rasquin, who was in Spain to seek aid, wrote to the King: "Those who remained in the city of Asunción when we left were more than fifty or sixty years old, and we left more than ten years ago . . . I am certain many of them are dead. . . ."[128]

In 1558, in the election of Francisco Ortiz de Zarate as governor, 359 Spaniards voted.[129] Ramirez de Quiñona wrote in 1566 that "there is a great necessity for aid for

[128] Quoted in Gandía, 1932c, p. 311.

[129] Gandía, in an editor's footnote to Díaz de Guzmán, 1943, p. 228. In the absence of appointments from Spain elections were sometimes held. Both Irala and Ortiz were elected governor.

that land [Paraguay] where there are three hundred Spaniards all of fifty years and older. . . ."[130] In 1569 Ortiz de Vergara, in reporting a census of Asunción, listed only 263 (Spanish) men as residents of Asunción.[131] Martín Gonzales, writing in 1575, said there were "no more than 280 Spaniards, 100 of them crippled, and the rest already old."[132] The Royal Cosmographer, López de Velasco, writing as of 1571-74, gave four hundred Spanish residents, "nearly all encomenderos," as the total for the three Spanish towns of Paraguay (Asunción, Villarrica, Ciudad Real).[133]

The diminution in numbers of true Spaniards was more than matched, however, by the growth of the mestizo population. In 1575 Martín Gonzales, the above-mentioned resident, could give the following information: ". . . in the city of Asunción alone there are 5,000 mestizos, more or less, sons of Spaniards and Indian women, and 3,000 of them are over 18 years of age, and there are another 5,000 mestizas [females] . . . ."[134] López de Velasco gave a smaller figure for the same period—four thousand mestizos (of both sexes) of ten to twenty-two years of age.[135] This professional cosmographer is more to be trusted than Gonzales, the man who accused some Spaniards of having eighty to one hundred Indian wives. In 1585 the treasurer of Río de la Plata, wrote that nine-tenths of the (non-Indian) population was mestizo, and that it was increasing so fast that in four years nearly one thousand boys would be born.[136]

The purely Indian population of Paraguay appears to have declined steadily throughout the latter half of the sixteenth century as a consequence of epidemics, wars, and, in the eastern part, slave raids of the Paulistas.[137] The polygynous relations of the encomenderos and Guaraní

[130] Ramírez de Quinoña: 1566, p. 210.

[131] Ortiz de Vergara: 1569, p. 97.

[132] Quoted in Torre Revello, 1943, p. 130.

[133] López de Velasco, 1894, p. 551.

[134] Quoted in Torre Revello, 1943, p. 130.

[135] López de Velasco, 1894, p. 551.

[136] Montalvo: 1585, p. 132.

[137] Hernández (1913, p. 123) said that in a space of 20 years the slave raiders took more than 300,000 Indians from Guayrá.

women also probably contributed to the diminution of the Indian population, for every Indian woman who bore children by a Spanish man correspondingly reduced the potential numbers of purely Indian births. By 1600 there were only three thousand Indians within a radius of seven leagues (over twenty-one miles) of Asunción.[138] As is stated later in this study, the encomiendas grew smaller throughout this period and their towns were often situated at great distances from Asunción.

By the end of the sixteenth century all the original Spanish conquerors must have died, and the first generation of half-breed mestizos probably had produced several thousand descendants. Of the second and third generations of mestizos, the majority probably had no more than one-quarter Spanish blood, for the Indian women continued to live in concubinage with mestizo encomenderos throughout this period.

These mestizos had a considerable measure of before-the-law equality with Spaniards and, apparently, considerable power which was a practical result of their numbers and their colonizing activity. Gandía has shown from documentary evidence that the conquerors in Paraguay had regarded the Guaraní as "gente de razón" and had intermarried chiefly with caciques' daughters and that Charles V sent a royal cedula which permitted sons of Spaniards and Guaraní to legally hold fiefs, canonships, and royal offices, "being descendants of caciques and nobility."[139]

The treasurer, Hernando de Montalvo, in a letter to the King in 1585, complained of the power of the mestizos, describing how, in the towns of the province which were outside of Asunción, the mestizos, by reason of their number, held the offices of alcaldes (mayors), regidores (councilmen), and major and minor alguaciles (constables).[140]

According to the Argentine historian, Ricardo Levene, the cabildo of Buenos Aires passed a resolution in 1589 on the question of rights to the wild horses, after a religious order had asked for them. The resolution states that: "It

[138] Métraux, 1948, p. 77.

[139] Gandía, 1939, p. 58. Azara (1923, 2:157, and 1943, p. 165) also stated that the mestizos were considered Spaniards.

[140] Montalvo: 1585, p. 140.

pertains to the children of the first conquerors to enjoy these wild horses as persons who inherited them from their fathers and as persons who sustain the said land at their own cost without being aided by his Majesty or any other person."[141]

Philip II, in 1579, had instructed Ortiz de Zarate that his encomienda could be inherited by his legitimate sons, and if there were none, his illegitimate children could inherit it with the same prerogative.[142] If his legitimate children were not mestizos, which is a limited possibility, his illegitimate ones certainly would be. It seems likely that the order to Ortiz was concerned particularly with the question of succession of encomiendas from legitimate to illegitimate children; whether they were mestizo was not of concern, else it would probably have been mentioned.[143]

There is abundant documentation which indicates that the mestizo sons of the conquerors were a very rebellious and individualistic group, lacking in humility toward their elders and toward political authority. According to Montalvo's letter to the King in 1579, "They are great friends of new things like the Indians," and "each day are getting more impudent and disrespectful. They commit crimes and are not punished."[144]

The Licentiate Cepeda, in 1591, wrote to the King describing the necessity of a governor of "age, goodness, courage, and experience," because the state of Paraguay and Río de la Plata is "so full of mestizos and delinquents . . . the creoles and mestizos . . . are usurping the

[141] Levene, 1937, pp. 42-43.

[142] "Yten os hacemos merced y demos facultad para que podais repartir y dar tierras y solares y cauallerias y estancias y otros sitios a todos vuestros hijos legitimos y naturales ansi en los pueblos que al presente estan poblados como los que aquí adelante se poblaren por vos el dicho juan ortiz y por vuestros capitanes y tenientes y en cuanto al repartimiento de los indios que como esta dicho aueis de tomar para vos en la dicha gouernacion lo podais dexar a vuestro hijo mayor legitimo o dividirlo en partes por los otros hijos legitimos que os pareciere y que falleciendo alguno do ellos puedan susceder y suscedan los demas que daren biuos en el dicho repartimiento y no teniendo hijos legitimos ningunos al tiempo de vuestro fin y muerte sucedan en el dicho repartimiento vuestros hijos o hijas naturales por la mesma orden y por la mesma prerrogativa que los legitimos." Gondra MS 515i.

[143] Ots Capdequí, 1934, p. 43.

[144] Montalvo: 1579, p. 106.

offices of justice . . . " and nothing good can come to "the land where such people rule. . . ."[145]

Gregorio de Acosta said: " . . . crimes of many of the mestizos are so frequent and so awful that I am ashamed to write of them to Your Majesty . . . they rob and defame whomever they wish . . . they carry off young women to the country and deflower and dishonor them . . . ."[146]

Father Rivadeneira described the mestizos as soldiers: "The boys who are old enough to carry a sword, they call 'club-boys' [mancebos de garrote], because, inasmuch as there are no swords, they carry long poles like half-lances. They are all very good men on horseback or on foot, because without shoes or pants they grow up like oaks, dextrous with their clubs, extremely beautiful shots, ingenious and curious and daring in war and even in peace; they are not very humble nor industrious at manual labor."[147]

However literally one may take these comments on the character of the mestizos in Paraguay, some things are clearly evident: (1) the Spaniards and the mestizos were beginning to feel antagonistic, as in other parts of the New World; (2) the mestizos in Paraguay, by virtue of sheer numerical predominance over the Spaniards, played an important role in colonization during the latter part of the sixteenth century and even held important offices; (3) they were already beginning to act rather more independently than the Spaniards liked.

Several mestizo uprisings or attempted rebellions occurred before 1600. Father Rivadeneira, whose comparatively balanced description has been quoted above, mentioned that there was an uprising planned by the mestizos in Asunción because they were not being given as many Indians in encomienda as they thought they deserved.[148]

In Buenos Aires in 1583, and twice in Santa Fé, in 1577 and 1580, mestizo uprisings occurred, and in Corrientes in 1588 the cabildo (town government) defied the governor and elected its own regidores.[149] Although these

[145] Cepeda: 1591, p. 116.

[146] Acosta: 1545, pp. 15-16.

[147] Gandía, 1932a, p. 99.

[148] Quoted in Gandía, 1932b. pp. 93-94.

[149] Levene, 1937, pp. 41-42.

incidents occurred outside of Paraguay, the towns had been recently settled by a few Spaniards and a majority of mestizos, all coming from Asunción.

The rebelliousness of the mestizos and their antipathy toward Spanish rule are related to subsequent political developments in Paraguay, for these small and scattered rebellions marked the beginnings of the "comunero" movements of the seventeenth and eighteenth centuries--movements which culminated in the independence of Paraguay.

From the point of view of Guaraní acculturation, the fact that mestizos were regarded legally as "Spaniards" and gradually replaced true Spaniards as encomenderos of Indians is very important. The ties of kinship between the encomendero and his Indians were thus stronger and more extensive, and linguistic barriers ceased to exist. There is also the probability that the cultural differences between the Indians and mestizos were progressively lessened, not only because of the acculturation of the Guaraní, but because the culture of the mestizo population had deviated in some ways from the customs of their fathers.

It is not possible to give in detail the specific changes which overtook the original Spanish culture by the time Spaniards were largely succeeded by mestizos, but it seems likely that they must have been extensive. The consequences of prolonged isolation probably altered many Spanish institutions, especially those most closely associated with subsistence activities. On the other hand, some customs and values may have retained their vigor. Isolation does not necessarily alter many of the less practical customs, but often seems to contribute in some way to their preservation. It is possible, however, to demonstrate that, coincidentally with the rise of mestizos, the encomiendas took on a local, specifically "Paraguayan" character. The course of the adaptation of the Guaraní Indians to Paraguayan life during the following period of permanent settlement was greatly influenced by the peculiar structure of the mitayo and originario encomiendas.

IV. THE COLONIAL PHASE: THE ORIGINARIO ENCOMIENDA

The transition from the exploratory phase of the settlement at Asunción to the phase of the stable "Paraguayan" colonial institutions was a period which covered perhaps one generation—from the time of the encomienda grants of 1556 until 1575 or 1580. By about 1580 the colony had taken on the most important local characteristics which were to influence life in later colonial Paraguay. The two forms of the encomienda, the originario and mitayo, were by this time flourishing institutions which retained their stability for the remainder of the colonial period.

The system of year-round personal service by Indian women and families of Indians had begun during the founding of Asunción and, despite the clerics' accusations of slavery and immorality, continued throughout the colonial period.[150] After Irala created the encomiendas this type of service came to be designated as "encomienda" also and was distinguished from the true encomienda of village Indians by the name "encomienda yanacona" or "encomienda originaria."

Azara, who described Paraguay and its history in the first years of the nineteenth century, said:

"The leaders in charge of the conquest of Paraguay and Río de la Plata established a distinction in the manner of treating the Indians. If they were guilty of insults or injustices toward the Spaniards, the Spaniards, after conquering them, divided them among each other as servants. There were also many Indians who requested, voluntarily and insistently, that the Spaniards take them as such servants. From this came the encomiendas called Yanaconas and Originarios. In these establishments each Spanish encomendero had the Indians continually with him, whatever their sex and age, and he used them as domestic servants in whatever way he found convenient. But he was prohibited from selling them, mistreating them, or dismissing them because of bad conduct, sickness, or old age, and he was obliged to clothe them, feed them, care for them in sickness, instruct them in religion and teach them an occupation. All this was verified by an inspector who annually heard the complaints of the Indians."[151]

[150] The following sources, which describe the originario system as of 1679, 1780, and 1801, present evidence that there was no significant change throughout the subsequent colonial period: Cédula Real: 1679; Pino Manrique: 1780; Azara, 1943, p. 168.

[151] Azara, 1923, 2:16-17. Azara is the only author who made a distinction between originario and yanacona. I shall follow the majority of sources by using originario for both.

Garay described the originario as composed of "peoples subjugated by individual force . . . [who] . . . were obliged to cultivate the lands of their encomenderos, and to hunt and fish for them. Their condition was like that of serfs, and the duty to work for their masters was not limited by age or sex, or anything except the wishes of the masters, although the servitude was generally softened by their goodness, as they had the obligation of protecting [the Indians] and instructing them in the Christian religion. . . . They did not have the right to sell the Indians, or mistreat them, or abandon them for bad behavior, sickness or old age." [152]

It is possible that Azara was the source for Garay's statements. At any rate, the remarks are similar enough to be considered together. Azara was anti-Jesuit and, as is evident, was inclined to portray the encomendero in a sympathetic light. He also apparently built his case on the evidence of the liberal humanitarian laws which were usually ineffective.

It is of some importance to note that the Indians in permanent servitude, the originarios, included, according to Azara, Indians captured in war, as well as Guaraní. [153] It is most difficult to decide what was the proportion of war captives in the originarios. Garay and Azara may have been inclined to emphasize their numbers because household servitude of captives of a "just war" was within the law. [154]

Documentary evidence indicates that the originarios were composed mostly, or perhaps entirely, of Guaraní. It was shown in Chapter II that in the first years of the colony it was the Guaraní who provided the women who lived with the Spaniards and served them. As Diego Téllez de Escobar described the institution in 1556, there is no word of war captives.[155] The Guaraní must have been

[152] Garay, 1942, p. 116.

[153] The question is somewhat complicated by testimony of the Jesuit writers who described the originario system of the early seventeenth century as consisting of Christian Indians and the mitayos as infidels. Gandía, 1939, p. 44.

[154] There were apparently instructions from Spain to Paraguay which permitted this, for Pedro Dorantes, in referring to the possibility of enslavement of some rebellious Agazes, mentioned "Royal Instructions" to this effect. Dorantes: n.d., pp. 128-31.

[155] Quoted on p. 37.

preferable as residents of the haciendas because the Indians of the Chaco had always shown themselves to be implacable enemies of the Spaniards and Guaraní. There is a wealth of evidence throughout the later encomienda phase of the colonization that a large number of Guaraní women were kept in the Spanish households and that polygyny remained the basis of the originario system. In fact, if conjectures of the numbers of women kept by the earlier colonists are correct, the system eventually included more women than it did in the exploratory period. Statements from the most reliable chroniclers of the period from 1579 until about 1630 show quite conclusively that out of the total population of nearly four thousand people in Asunción, there were about ten women to every man.[156]

A consideration of the ordinances of several governors during this period indicates that Guaraní women were taken continually from the mitayo pueblos to serve in the Spanish households and estates. Successive decrees of the governors Irala, Ramírez, and Hernandarias, and the inspector, Alfaro, made in the years 1556, 1597, 1603, and 1611, respectively, all were attempts to limit the practice of procuring women from the Indian villages. The fact that they all prohibited the same acts is an indication that the laws must have been ineffective.

The way in which some of the ordinances were written is instructive, for they are often descriptive of the situation. One of Ramírez' several ordinances on this subject states: "I am informed that Spanish residents of the pueblos publicly have Indian girls . . . as concubines." Another ordinance says: "Because the encomenderos have taken servants in an unregulated manner, and the pueblos

[156] In 1579 Montalvo reported to the King that there were 2,500 women in the city of Asunción (Montalvo: 1579, p. 106). Governor Ramírez de Velasco's ordinances of 1597 gave the population of Asunción as 200 men and 2,000 women (Ramírez de Velasco: 1597, ordinance 41). The Jesuit chronicler, Ruiz de Montoya, writing of the first half of the seventeenth century, said that Asunción had 4,000 residents, and it was "commonly said that for one man there were ten women" (Ruiz de Montoya, 1892, p. 16). The discrepancy between this figure and the 2,200 given above possibly occurred because Governor Ramírez did not include children. León Pinelo gave 400 men and 4,000 women (León Pinelo, 1943, 2:497). Despite the differences in the estimates of total population, these men all agreed that during the latter sixteenth and early seventeenth centuries the proportion of women to men was ten to one.

are thus dissipated . . . I order that . . . no encomendero may take for personal service any Indian woman who is married, because of the notable harm, particularly if she has children."

Some of Hernandarias' ordinances are similarly revealing: " . . . experience shows that the [mitayo] encomiendas are being used up because the encomenderos take away members of it. . ." and, "I am aware that among the encomenderos and many other persons . . . there is great lack of prudence in having concubines among the Indian women of their service."[157]

Evidence from 1677 indicates that concubinage continued through the period following Alfaro's attempts to abolish the originario system. Reje Gorvalán recounted in a letter to the King that the Indian women of the originarios were used sexually by the encomendero and by his sons as well.[158]

The statements of Garay and Azara that originario Indians were war captives seem to bear little relation to actuality, and their failure to mention polygyny as one of the bases of the system also distorts the picture. Many documentary sources also disagree with Azara's implication that the encomenderos took such good care of their Indians that they instructed them in religion, taught them an occupation, and so on.

For example, a Jesuit, Diego de Torres, in 1609, complained of the mistreatment of these Indians, saying that they were like slaves, without much food, and were not being taught the Catholic doctrine.[159] Juán del Pino Manrique, Protector of the Indians, in a report on encomiendas in 1780, gave a description and a historical sketch

[157]The particular ordinances which deal with this situation are as follows: Irala: 1556a, ordinances 2 and 3; Ramírez de Velasco: 1597, ordinances 13, 28, 32, 34; Hernandarias de Saavedra: 1603, ordinances 11, 20, 21; Alfaro: 1611, ordinances 18, 25, 35.

[158]"Permitenlas primero estar amancebadas, con yndios de otras encomiendas por valerse de su Travajo que los matrimonios olvidados del temor de Dios y de la falta que haran en su origen quedando por esta rason tan opresos y desconsolados cuanto se deja entender con otros graves encombenientes y pecados que se ocasionan viviendo las yndias de puertas adentro con sus encomenderos de que Resulta tener sus hijos ocasion pincua de aprovecharse de la facilidad de las chinas saciando su libiandad y aun sus mismos padres padeciendo sus legitimas mugeres no haciendo caso de ellas y estan general este dano." Gondra MS 1036.

[159]Cartas Anuas, 1927-29, 19:9.

of the encomiendas of that day which conflicted considerably with the rather rosy accounts of Garay and Azara:

"The Indians of this Province [Paraguay] are divided into two classes of encomiendas according to the principle adhered to since the times of the conquest; those that form towns and have their own land where they live together assisted by a parish priest and a Spanish administrator . . . or commonly only the priest himself, and others that do not live in towns and do not have their own lands, but pass from one encomendero to another, living always in their houses, estancias or farms.

"[The Indians] that do not have their own land or villages are distinguished by the name of orijinarios. . . .

"The unhappy continuation of the cruel servitude that these miserable people suffer exceeds that of slaves . . . when a resident acquires an encomienda of orijinarios he believes he has bought a family of slaves, whose procreation augments the number of slaves of both sexes, with the difference that he cannot sell them, nor leave them by inheritance to his sons . . . a circumstance which exposes the miserable Indians to greater hardships, so that what appears to be a privilege compared to the situation of slaves, causes them to suffer greater hardships than if they actually were. . . .

"The orijinarios are born, live, and die in the houses of their encomendero, or in their estancias and farms. It is few [encomenderos] who, with any care, teach them the Christian doctrine. . . ."[160]

It is evident that, whatever importance one may wish to attach to such complaints, not everybody agreed that the actual situation was quite the one described by Azara. It is difficult, and probably profitless, to attempt to make a general statement of whether Indian life as an originario was heaven or hell. Probably some Indians were well treated and others were not. Most writers were partisan in their defense of this system or opposition to it because the question of personal service was an important one in those days, and the originario was a system of personal service in its ultimate realization. It is of significance to note, however, that Francisco de Alfaro, the great opponent of the originario system, made a statement which indicates

[160] Pino Manrique: 1780.

that the Paraguayan Indians under this system did not consider themselves badly treated. Article 57 of his ordinances sought to end personal service and substitute tribute in its place, and in this article he mentioned the difficulty of abolishing personal service "because most of the Indians, in the inspections I have made, especially in the city of Asunción, say they do not want to pay tribute; some . . . because they do not know what it is; others because they say they serve whenever and however they wish and the Spaniards give them gifts; others [say] that they help the Spaniards, not by way of tribute nor servitude, but as relatives. . . ."[161] This statement does not serve Alfaro's purpose as an opponent of the Paraguayan system, by any means. His reason for making it was to explain the difficulty in enforcing his ordinances because neither Spaniards nor Indians wanted tribute to replace personal service.

The poverty of the originario Indians must have been miserable for, as has been mentioned, the Indians were not paid for their labor until Alfaro attempted to institute free wage labor in 1611. Ramírez de Velasco's ordinance 12 states: "Inasmuch as it has been customary for the Indians who serve in the cities to go about naked because of their poverty and misery . . . I order that every year the encomenderos shall have each married Indian plant 200 cotton plants with which to dress his family. . . ."[162] Hernandarias appears to have been concerned with the same thing, for his ordinance 17 requires that the encomendero give one set of clothing every year to each of the men and women of his personal service.[163]

There is lack of conclusive evidence as to the inheritance of originario Indians. Ordinance 27 of Hernandarias seems to indicate that the originario followed the usual two generation encomienda rule, at least up to the time this ordinance was published in 1603. The ordinance is extracted as follows:

"In these provinces it is customary and evident each day that when an encomendero dies and his encomienda, because it is in the second generation of inheritance, is

[161]Alfaro: 1611.

[162]Ramírez de Velasco: 1597.

[163]Hernandarias: 1603.

vacant [belongs to no one], the wife and sons are lost and there is no remedy--a thing of great sorrow and pity. Therefore, . . . I order that from now on [in such a case], the Indians of personal service of his farms and estancias shall remain on those of the sons because of desire and love that they have always shown by serving him. They shall stay in the said farms and estancias of the oldest son, and if there are no sons, the wife of the above encomendero shall have them. If there are neither, the Indians may choose to stay or may go to other masters . . . ."[164]

There is evidence, however, that considerable anarchy and lack of regulation were usual in the inheritance of these servants. The statement that the Indians might "choose" to go or stay certainly bore little relation to reality. Pedro Dorantes, writing to the Council of the Indies in 1573, told of "Pedro de Espinar, who died . . . leaving fields, cows, cattle, [etc.] . . . . On his farm he had more than 50 servants, whom he declared in his testament to be free, and who could, if they wished, stay on his farm and have his tools that were necessary to sustain themselves there. Felipe de Cazares took them all. . . ." In the same letter Dorantes said that on the death of an encomendero the servants were left to the sons, but if there were no sons, whoever was in command took them or gave them away as he wished.[165]

Captain Martín de Orue, in a letter to the King in 1573, wrote: "The Indians . . . who live on the estancias and estates of the Spaniards. . . . . . . are benefited greatly and are multiplying, they ennoble and populate the land, the Spaniards are more comfortable, and they make mills and cattle estancias. . . . All this ceases to be because those who govern rule that when a Spaniard dies who has no sons, his servants whom he has raised are taken away and divided, a father given away one place, the mother another, and the children to another, and against their will. . . ."[166]

The ordinances reveal other matters of interest about the originario system. For example, the hours and days

[164] Ibid.

[165] Dorantes: 1573, pp. 138-39.

[166] Orue: 1573, p. 165.

of work had apparently been unregulated except by the encomendero's own desires. Ramírez de Velasco stated:

"And because in this state there is no order nor standard for the Indians' work and the said encomenderos are served by them with great lack of regulation, working them all the year and even the [sacred days], making them work in the fields and jobs in their towns as well as in the cities, causing them much harm . . . I order that . . . the citizens of the cities must not be served [by the Indians] more than four days each week, Monday, Tuesday, Wednesday, Thursday. Fridays and Saturdays they must be allowed to work in their own fields . . . and fiesta days they must not work. . . ."

Another ordinance complains that Indian manpower has been used to operate flour mills, and commands that the mills henceforth be operated by wind or water.

Hernandarias, in the introductory statements to his ordinances of 1603, stated that "there has been great lack of regulation in the treatment of the Indians" and dismissed previous laws as having worked more for the utility of the encomendero than for the conservation of the Indians. He ordered that personal servants be given no work on Sunday, so that they might hear Mass, adding: "I have seen many irregularities in making the Indian men and women work on fiesta days."[167]

Alfaro's decrees summarily attempted to abolish personal service altogether and substitute wage labor in its place; thus his ordinances cannot be compared with the others on specific points. The fact that the same ordinances are repeated so often attests to their ineffectiveness and proves that unregulated labor performed at the whim of the encomendero was usual.

There was little real attempt to indoctrinate the originario Indians to the extent which the Crown considered proper. It was common for them to have to work on fiesta days and Sundays, as has been shown. Ramírez de Velasco attempted to remedy the lack of religious instruction by ordering that each encomendero should have on his estate two boys and two girls who knew the doctrine, in order

[167]The several ordinances mentioned above are: Ramírez de Velasco: 1597, ordinances 7, 23; Hernandarias de Saavedra: 1603, ordinances 9, 10.

that they might teach the Indian men and women, who were to be brought together each night to hear evening prayers. Hernandarias also ordered the encomendero to give religious instruction to the Indians in his personal service. Many of Alfaro's later ordinances likewise indicate his dissatisfaction with the failure of encomenderos to indoctrinate the Indians.[168] One of the causes of this state of affairs was the notable lack of clerics during the whole period from the conquest until the time of the Jesuits. In fact, this is one of the reasons why the Jesuits were finally asked to come to Paraguay.[169]

Some encomenderos had farms and ranches where originario Indians remained the year around, isolated from contact with churches. Ramírez de Velasco ordered that: "Inasmuch as many encomenderos have their estancias away from the pueblos of their encomiendas, and have many Indian men and women in them who do not hear Mass all year . . . and live in ignorance . . . and die without confession. . . . I order that every 15 days half of the Indians be taken to the city or nearest parish to hear Mass. . . ." Hernandarias made a similar statement six years later: "I order that all citizens be obliged to send the Indians of their farms and estancias to hear Mass on Sundays and fiesta days, leaving always someone to guard the herds . . . and every night they should hear the Christian doctrine. . . ."[170]

The isolated farms alluded to could not have been very large, as there were no cash crops of consequence in Paraguay, and the cattle estancias also must have been small. The Indians serving on them were probably not numerous and were apparently quite isolated. As a result, they probably did not figure importantly in the formation of Paraguayan culture. Those who eventually returned from such isolated estancias to their own pueblos may have had some effect on the village Indians, assuming they taught their knowledge of Spanish animal husbandry, but they were outside the main influences which affected the originarios.

[168] Ramírez de Velasco: 1597, ordinance 17; Hernandarias de Saavedra: 1603, ordinances 4, 9, 10; Alfaro: 1611, ordinance 7.

[169] Azara, 1923, 2:120.

[170] Ramírez de Velasco: 1597, ordinance 16; Hernandarias: 1603, ordinance 7.

There is virtually no information on the workings of the originario in the Spanish settlements of Villarrica and Ciudad Real in the remote Paraná region. It is likely that, because of greater isolation, the encomenderos were even more lax with respect to laws and regulations than in Asunción, if that be possible. The little evidence available suggests that the originario system of the Paraná region was probably similar to that of Asunción with the exceptions that more Indians were involved and that the poverty and lack of religious instruction which characterized Asunción were, if anything, even greater in Guayrá.

As has been noted in Chapter III, the Indians were very numerous and the Spaniards comparatively few. The Royal Cosmographer, López de Velasco, writing of the period 1571-74, said there were in Ciudad Real eighty to one hundred residents, nearly all with encomienda Indians, "of which there are many in this locality."[171] Vásquez de Espinosa visited Paraguay in the 1620's, and described Villarrica as follows: ". . . in that wretched country, with the extreme poverty of the Spaniards living there, they have no priests to administer the Holy Sacraments, and so they are like savages without a country, never hearing Mass, and their children go seven or eight years without being christened. . . . The Spaniards living here are so poor that their only clothes are of cotton and they wear palm-leaf hats, for no Spanish merchandise ever gets here, and they have nothing with which to buy any."[172]

It would be difficult to invent a system of exploitation which could be more conducive to thorough acculturation of the Indians than the Paraguayan originario system. The Guaraní were so completely dominated by the Spaniards that many aspects of their lives could be altered at the whim of the encomendero. Legalistic attempts at control were ineffective, and the Spaniards used the Indians in any way they wished, but there is evidence that this situation was somewhat moderated because of the prevalence of kinship ties between the encomendero and his Indians, so that from the Indians' point of view the exploitation was not necessarily cruel or unnatural. In addition, the fact that the Paraguayan economy did not permit a cash crop plantation system possibly limited the degree of harsh exploitation

[171] López de Velasco, 1894, p. 557.

[172] Vásquez de Espinosa, 1942, p. 687.

of the Indians. Nevertheless, it would have been difficult for the Indians to retain much cultural independence in matters incompatible with the encomendero's interests.

The year-round residence of the Indians on the encomenderos' lands naturally altered many aspects of aboriginal culture. There could have been no village organization, and the aboriginal division of labor by sex must have been modified, as men were used more and more for new kinds of labor. The few native specializations of labor must also have been altered somewhat.

The kinship system and marriage customs probably were changed in some ways, even though Paraguayan culture retained some of the basic aboriginal features, such as polygyny and kinship labor obligations. The few Indians who lived together under one encomendero must have been only a part of a complete aboriginal lineage, and extended kin ties, with their reciprocal obligations, were therefore weakened to the extent that a lineage was divided among separate encomenderos. An additional weakening factor, after one generation, was that many members of an extended lineage were mestizos, who probably felt a social distinction between themselves and their pure Indian relatives. Only a small proportion of mestizos could have succeeded to their fathers' estates, and the social and economic position of the remainder is not known, but it seems likely that they did not consider themselves on exactly the same social plane as their Indian cousins even if they were in a similar economic status.

The close association of Indians with the Spaniards is obviously a favorable circumstance for the transmission of cultural elements, especially the many skills learned by the Indian laborers and servants. This association must also have had an effect on the Spanish culture, for some useful features of Guaraní culture were taken over by the Spaniards. The rapid adoption of the pattern of native polygyny and kinship labor obligations is a case in point. Other obvious examples are the use of the basic native crops, techniques for raising them, and cooking and child rearing customs. As time passed, both Spanish and Indian culture were probably progressively modified in ways which lessened the gulf between them.

By the time mestizos became the basic "Spanish" population and were encomenderos of Indians, the original

Spanish culture had incorporated many Guaraní elements into a rather distinctively "Paraguayan" culture. In addition to the blending of Spanish and Indian subsistence and economic traits, many minor Guaraní habits and customs probably became a part of colonial culture as a result of polygyny. The large number of mestizo children associated with their Guaraní mothers and Indian relatives for informal day-to-day education more often than they would have as members of a small monogamous family. Many items of Guaraní folklore and superstition were probably passed on in this way. The retention of the Guaraní language by the mestizos was also a consequence of this kind of daily association.

Evidence of the ambitions of the mestizos seems to indicate that many purely Spanish attitudes and values were imparted to them by their encomendero fathers. These values were probably mostly derived from the older Spanish feudal ideology rather than from the newer middle-class ideals which were growing stronger in Spain at the time of the conquest of the New World, for the subsistence economy of Paraguay fostered the retention of the former at the expense of the values of the trading class. This is of significance for Indian acculturation, inasmuch as the communal basis of Indian values seems usually to be more compatible with feudalism than with the ideology of a commercial economy.

Under mestizo encomenderos relations between master and workers were probably closer than under the pure Spaniards. The bilingual and somewhat bicultural mestizos could be capable of considerably more understanding of Guaraní customs. In addition, the continued polygyny of mestizos and Indian women now may have often added blood ties to the usual affinal relationship between Indians and their encomendero and thus strengthened the adherence of many Guaraní socioeconomic patterns to Paraguayan culture. Status polygyny, the agricultural role of women, and labor obligations of the kin group all appear to have been an important part of the Paraguayan system under the mestizos.

The continued scarcity of ecclesiastics still left the encomendero as the most important source of religious instruction of the originario Indians. Evidence has suggested that the Spaniards did not attend to these duties and that the mestizo progeny was notably irreligious. It seems likely that after the mestizos became encomenderos religious instruction of the Indians must have amounted to very little. Under these circumstances, following generations of mestizos would become successively even less religious, unless formal religious schools later remedied the situation.

V. THE COLONIAL PHASE: THE MITAYO ENCOMIENDA

The mitayo encomienda, unlike the originario, extended Spanish control and influence to Indian villages which were far from Asunción and brought Indians who had been relatively unacculturated during the exploratory phase of the colonization into a regulated colonial system. The formal structure of this encomienda is of more relevance in considering Guaraní acculturation than was that of the originario, for the relations between Spaniards and Guaraní were more impersonal, and the Indians were less subject to continual surveillance by their encomendero, except during the periods of labor service. The Indians retained the integrity of their social units longer because they still lived together and tilled their own village lands. Thus, their culture was altered less as a consequence of breakdown than of slower modification. Although the mitayo system allowed the Indians less independence than the Crown desired, the Indians were, nevertheless, more protected than in the originario system. Their acculturation has to be judged chiefly in the light of the probable functional consequences of the form of the mitayo system on a particular kind of Indian culture.

The Size of Mitayo Encomiendas

The Paraguayan mitayo encomiendas were not large at the time of their inception in 1556, and they became even smaller as the purely Indian population in the vicinity of Asunción declined during the first one hundred years of the colony. The first concrete reference to numbers is Governor Irala's previously cited statement that twenty thousand

Indians were placed in the first encomiendas. It must be assumed that this number included all of the available Indians of the vicinity, for there was a great deal of dissatisfaction with the small size of the encomiendas. Had they been divided equally among the 320 Spaniards, each encomienda would have totaled sixty-two or sixty-three Indians. They were not, of course, thus equally divided. Juán de Salazar, one of the captains of the Mendoza expedition and the founder of Asunción, received "not even 200 Indians."[173] Because of his relatively high rank, his encomienda may be assumed to be one of the larger ones.

A statement by Pedro Dorantes to the Council of the Indies indicates something of the size of encomiendas: "In the report that I made to the Royal Council in the year '56 I told how the Governor Domyngo de Yrala . . . made a great number of encomiendas and that they were a great injury to the natives because a man with 30 or 40 Indians given to him wanted to accomplish as much as another with 300, and that it seemed to me that they should be reduced to a much smaller number [of encomiendas]. . ."[174]

There were, of course, plenty of Indians in Paraguay, especially in the Chaco, but these Indians were unremitting enemies of the Spaniards, and apparently it was impossible to subdue them. López de Velasco noted that in 1571-74 there were more than four hundred thousand Indians in the region of Asunción;[175] however, it must be assumed that most of them were across the Paraguay River in the Chaco wilderness.

Azara listed forty Indian towns formed between 1536 and 1610,[176] but they were widely scattered. Pastells, writing of the period just before 1612, said that there were one thousand mitayo Indians in three towns within six or seven leagues (about seventeen miles [177]) of Asunción.[178] Since the Spaniards brought the mita Indians from much farther away than this, there must have been many more

[173]Salazar: 1556, p. 581.

[174]Dorantes: 1573, pp. 138-39.

[175]López de Velasco, 1894, p. 556.

[176]Azara, 1923, 2:129.

[177]In Paraguay a league was 2.69 miles. Haggard and McLean, 1941, p. 78.

[178]Quoted in Gandía, 1939, pp. 44-45.

mitayo Indians. According to the evidence of Ramírez de Velasco's ordinance 8, mita Indians came to Asunción to work from forty leagues away (one hundred miles) and more.[179]

Vásquez de Espinosa mentioned that in 1623 there were "250 encomenderos of Indians,"[180] and Ruiz de Montoya, writing of roughly the same period, said that Villarrica had 130 residents with nine pueblos of Indians in its jurisdiction.[181]

From these meager notes it is difficult to draw any accurate conclusions as to the numbers of Indians in the mitayo encomiendas. About the only permissible decision is that each pueblo must have been divided among several encomenderos, inasmuch as there were 250 encomenderos in Asunción alone. Assuming that there might have been twenty-five Indian villages as the maximum number within range of Asunción, this would mean that a pueblo contained an average of ten encomiendas. The usual encomienda probably contained a maximum of fifty Indians.[182]

Alfaro noted this situation in an illuminating passage which seems to indicate that, sometimes at least, there were as many as fifty encomiendas in a single village. This would suggest encomiendas considerably smaller than the estimated size: "Although I should like to levy taxes on each particular village [of mitayo Indians], I have not been able up to now for the following reasons: because in each village there are Indians of different encomenderos; most of them of such small number that they are not worth consideration. Because even in this city of Asunción, capital of the country, there are many who do not have even ten encomienda Indians. And I have visited villages, large enough for a mission, in which I found Indians belonging to fifty encomenderos."[183]

179 Ramírez de Velasco: 1597.

180 Vásquez de Espinosa, 1942, p. 682.

181 Ruíz de Montoya, 1892, pp. 150-51.

182 Vásquez de Espinosa, in naming six Indian villages, mentioned the population of three of them as 400, 500, and 600 (quoted on p. 80). It would serve no purpose to calculate the average number of Indians in an encomienda from the figures given, because their accuracy cannot be trusted, but it can easily be seen that fifty is a high estimate.

183 Alfaro: 1611, ordinance 60.

There were many complaints about the small encomiendas, which support our suppositions, however unsatisfactory they may be statistically. Alfaro's ordinances of 1611, which substituted tribute in place of mita labor, elicited a storm of protests from those who repeatedly pointed out that the tributes in produce could not possibly suffice to sustain an encomendero because there were so few encomienda Indians.

In 1612 the cabildo of Asunción wrote to the King, requesting permission to bring Negroes from Angola or Brazil because the encomienda Indians were so few and so little work was done by them.[184] Captain Manuel de Frías, procurador general of the provinces, also wrote in 1617 of the necessity of importing Negroes, although he was referring to Argentina as well as Paraguay. In speaking of the lack of Indian labor, he said that many natives had died in the pestilence of 1605 and 1606.[185]

Pedro de Toro, in 1618, also submitted detailed objections to Alfaro's ordinances and added that there were not enough Indians, nor were there Indian slaves, mulat-

[184]". . . y si pareciere convenir para descargo de la real conciencia de Vuestra Magestad que se camine con el thenor de las ordenancas que dexo hechas el licensiado don francisco de alfaro sin embargo de los yncovienientas que se apuntan vasallos de Vuestra Magestad somos y los mas umildes subjetos que Vuestra Magestad tiene y asi suplicamos umilmente a Vuestra Magestad se sirva mandar que esto se vea con la atencion que el caso rrequiere teniendo considerasion a que quando se nos conceda; esta merced que pretendemos son tan pocos los yndios rredusidos y tan poco dados al travajo que no podemos pasar con sola su ayuda no sirviendose Vuestra Magestad de concedernos liciencia para que podamos traer de angola o del brasil negros con que comodamente nos podamos sustentar de gananes para crias y simenteras con que los derechos de ellos los paguemos en fructos de la tierra dentro de algunos placos favorables y a menos que esto no podia yr esta tierra adelante ni nosotros tener fuercas para continuar en el rreal servicio . . ." Gondra MS 1442.

[185]"El capitan Manuel de frias, Procurador general de las provincias del Rio de la plata y paraguay dize que el tiene pedido y suplicado a su magestad en nombre de las ocho ciudades dellas se sirva concederles liciencia para que por algunos anos puedan llevar de angola y del brasil la cantidad de esclavos contenida en su pedimiento por ser una de las cossas mas importantes para el rremedio y conservacion de los vesinos y moradores de las dichas ciudades para que con ellas se puedan ayudar en la labranca y crianca y para levantar y rreparar sus cassas y templos . . . atento a la gran falta de servicio que en aquella tierra ay por averse acavado y muerto muy gran suma de naturales con las pestes pasadas [of 1605 and 1606] . . ." Gondra MS 38a.

toes, or wage workers.[186] Fray Lujan de Medina and several associates wrote from Asunción in 1612 on the impossibility of applying tribute, saying that many citizens had not even ten Indians.[187] Bartólome Fernández, in 1618, wrote the Council of the Indies that tribute from the encomiendas would not be enough because the encomiendas consisted of only six, ten, twenty, or thirty Indians.[188]

By 1640 Alfaro's ordinances had long ceased to have any effect, and personal service of the Indians had been officially re-established, but reports from Paraguay continued to stress the small size of the encomiendas. Three documents are cited from this period. They are supplied as additional evidence because the documents quoted above were all written as objections to Alfaro's ordinances, and consequently one might suspect that their authors had exaggerated in arguing their case.

In 1639 Sebastián de León wrote to the King that the great merits and labors of the descendants of the conquistadors had not been rewarded by more than small encomiendas of Indians who worked in their corn, wheat, and sugar cane fields. All those products were used up in sustaining life and were barely sufficient to provide clothing.[189]

Orue de Zarate and several padres wrote in 1643 that the encomienda Indians were used only for help in cultivating the soil and were so few that the encomendero himself had to work in the fields.[190] A petition sent to the lieutenant general of Paraguay in 1640 stated that some encomiendas contained no more than two or three Indians.[191]

[186] Fernández: 1618, p. 517.

[187] Lujan de Medina: 1612, p. 459.

[188] Fernández: 1618, p. 513.

[189] The descendants of the conquerors ". . . cuyos méritos servicios y travaxos no an tenido mas satisfaccion que una pequena encomienda de Indios que solo an servido y sirven para las labores de las chacras de maiz trigo y cana y algunas pocas de vinas que todo se gasta y consume en el sustento umano y apenas ahorra un bestido para si." Gondra MS 209a.

[190] ". . . los que tambien sirven a su magestad se les da en alguna parte de remuneracion una encomienda muy tenua de yndios de los pocos que an quedado las quales no sir ven mas que de ayudar a cultivar la tierra a sus encomenderos para vestirlos aellos y propagar la doctrina y son de tan poco numero que los yndios de tan poco travajo y codicia que es necesario que el mismo encomendero are y travaxe y cultive la tierra . . ." Gondra MS 209c.

[191] ". . . las encomiendas son de tan poco numero que ay encomienda

It is difficult to account exactly for the scarcity of Guaraní Indians available to Asunción. Documents mention widespread epidemics at two separate intervals in Paraguay. López de Velasco said that in 1558 or 1560 there was a pestilence which did not harm the Spaniards but which killed more than one hundred thousand Indians;[192] and Manuel de Frías mentioned one in 1605-6 which killed a great number of Indians.[193] It is also possible that numbers of Indians had fled to the hills of Guayrá. The continued concubinage of Indian women increased the mestizo population at the expense of the pure Indians and thus also accounted for some of the decrease in Indian population.

Since the usual Crown policy that encomiendas of Indians were to be free after two generations of Spaniards had held them was not observed in Paraguay, this cannot be considered a cause of the diminution in numbers of encomienda Indians. Alfaro and the Council of the Indies attempted to establish the freedom of all the encomienda Indians who were supposed to be free under the two generation rule, but although this ordinance was observed in Buenos Aires, Santa Fé, and Corrientes, it received no attention in Paraguay.[194]

In Paraguay the right of the first adelantados to grant encomiendas was retained by subsequent governors,[195] and although an encomienda might belong to a family for only the legal two generations, once it was free, the governor would grant it again to someone he considered worthy. Even Philip II gave his permission to Governor Ortiz de Zarate in 1579 to make a grant of that nature although the practice was already an accomplished fact. Philip also allowed the encomiendas to be given for three generations.[196]

que apenas tienen dos o tres yndios y con ellos tan tas cargas y obligaciones y los oficios de ningun provecho por la comun pobreza de la tierra y por que el tiempo que los sirven pierden sus chacras y haciendas con que se sustentan Assi y a sus mugeres y hijos que es menester travajar de nuevo y entablar lo pedido porque son de solo frutos . . ." Gondra MS 209d.

[192]López de Velasco, 1894, p. 552.

[193]Gondra MS 38a, copied in footnote 185.

[194]Azara, 1943, p. 168; Lastarría, 1914, pp. 28-29.

[195]León Pinelo, 1922, p. 101.

[196]"Yten os damos poder y facultad para que podais repartir y encomendar en la dicha gouernacion todos los indios y encomiendas que

It is probable that the small number of Indians was a circumstance which contributed indirectly to their acculturation. As the proportion of Indians to encomenderos grew smaller, the amount of personal control over individual Indians was probably increased; Spaniards and Indians were thus in closer and more frequent contact. The decrease in village population also must have contributed to the disruption of the native village organization, a circumstance which normally weakens the resistance of a culture to outside acculturative influence.

Village Organization

The Guaraní Indians, in their aboriginal condition, lived in extended family kin groups in small villages, the location of which they shifted every few years because their agricultural methods tended to exhaust the soil. One of the important effects of Spanish control on their culture was the change caused by grouping the Indians into larger and permanent villages, "reducing" them to easier control and indoctrination. In attempting to describe these towns from the few sketchy references available, it is necessary to note the date of each reference, because the house type and organization of Indian villages were almost necessarily exposed to considerable change over a period of time.

López de Velasco, royal cosmographer, described the Paraguayan encomienda towns of 1571-74 as follows: "The [Indians] are all in little towns of 100 to 200 or less population, in some houses or large huts made of straw, 400 or 500 paces in length [the towns, it must be supposed].

estouieren bacos y bacaren de aqui adelante asi en las ciudades y pueblos que al presente estan poblados y se poblaren de aquiadelante en la dicha gouernacion asi por vos el dicho juan ortiz de carate como por vuestros capitanes y lugares tenientes y encomendar los dichos repartimientos en esta manera en los pueblos que al presente es tan poblados en la dicha gouernacion por dos vidas conforme a la sucesion y orden que tenemos dada en los dichos repartimientos y en los pueblos que de aqui adelante se poblaren por os hac r mas merced y a las petsomas que os ayudaren a conquistar poblar la tierra y poblarla os damos facultad para que podais encomendar los indios por tres vidas que se entiende por la vida de aquel en quien primero se hiciere la tal encomienda y para sui hijo y nieto / ASI baron como hembra prefiriendose siempre en esta sucexion al baron a la hembra y en defecto de no tener hijo ni nieto que suceda su misma mujer conforme a lo ordenado." Gondra MS 515i.

They are all in encomiendas, without having to pay any tribute, and they serve their encomendero in their turn by doing his work."[197]

By 1620 some of the towns seem to have had much larger populations. Vásquez de Espinosa named several encomienda villages: "Round about in its neighborhood, the city [Asunción] has many Indian villages, like Elita, a Franciscan parish with 500 Indians; Yaguarón, with 400, Los Altos, Tobatí, all reasonable Indians; Tuyabacobá, which means old man without a face; Yutí, a village of over 600 Indians, catechized by the Jesuit Fathers; Guarambaré, and many others."[198]

It is possible that at first the Indians were not regrouped and placed into new and larger villages at all, but were required to remain in their original villages. Irala's ordinances of 1556 had provided that the Indians must remain permanently in their villages, a rule which was undoubtedly enforced. This implies a certain amount of change in Indian customs, for the aboriginal agricultural methods must have been altered by some means which allowed permanent use of land.

The Spaniards' control over the settlement pattern must have been fairly complete, for later they sometimes arbitrarily moved a whole village. R. I. Cardozo described a few of these movements in his discussion of the history of Villarrica:

". . . in 1575 Villa Rica del Espíritu Santo [was founded] by Ruy Díaz de Melgarejo, 50 leagues above Ciudad Real, on the Paranapané, at the mouth of the Huibai. Later it was moved near the Curumbatay River, a tributary of the former, from where, because of the frequent incursions of the mamelucos of San Pablo, the Lieutenant Governor of the Province, don Martín de Ledesma changed its location in 1635, locating it to the East of Jejuí, near the Curuguatí River, in a place called Tupaitá, by virtue of a Royal Cedula. In this movement, the residents took with them the Indian encomienda towns of San Pedro de Terecañí, San Francisco de Ivapariyará, Nuestra Señora de la Candelaria, and San Andrés de Mbaracayú, and established them in the new residence,

197 López de Velasco, 1894, p. 555.

198 Vásquez de Espinosa, 1942, p. 683.

Terecañí on the Jejuí, Candelaria on the Curaguaté, and Ivapariyará to the east of Acaray."[199]

Similar movements occurred with other Indian villages. According to Azara, Ipané, Guarambaré, Atira, Tobatí, Yutý, Loreto, and San-Ignacio-Miri were all moved at one time or another.[200]

Azara also noted that each of the villages had a political life that was modeled on that of the Spanish towns. Each pueblo had an Indian corregidor (Crown representative), and two alcaldes and regidores.[201] Although this may have been true of the encomienda towns of Azara's time--the beginning of the nineteenth century--it does not seem to have been true before 1611. Irala's ordinances of 1556 state that the Indians must obey their caciques (native chiefs) but make no other provision for political officers in the pueblos. Ramírez de Velasco's ordinances of 1597 likewise contain no references to such political officers. Hernandarias, in 1603, ordered that each pueblo having as many as one hundred Indians should have a fiscal (a sort of public prosecutor), and those with over one hundred Indians should have two. It is evident from the context of his remarks in another ordinance that the duties of the fiscal were to teach the doctrine and see that the Indians went to church. He did not provide for any other political offices.

Alfaro, the newcomer who was always so zealous that his ordinances should rigidly reflect the Crown policy, was the first actually to make provisions for the Spanish type of political officers. His 1611 ordinances state that each pueblo should have an Indian alcalde and that if there were more than eighty houses, there should be two alcaldes and two regidores; if there were many houses, there should be four of each.[202]

It is not possible to say whether Alfaro's ordinances caused the encomenderos to establish these officers in the pueblos. Before 1611, however, control of the Indian villages was clearly in the hands of the encomenderos, who

199 R. I. Cardozo, 1938a, p. 128.

200 Azara, 1923, 2:188-97.

201 Ibid., 1943, p. 166.

202 The ordinances referred to are: Hernandarias de Saavedra: 1603, ordinances 6, 8; Irala: 1556a, ordinance 1; Alfaro: 1611, ordinance 8.

apparently worked through the caciques in certain matters. As has been seen, Irala ordered in 1556 that the Indians obey their caciques, and Ramírez indicated that the caciques were supposed to be responsible for seeing that the Indians served in the mita labor at the required time. The sons of the caciques were to be occupied in teaching the doctrine to the rest of the Indians. Both Ramírez and Hernandarias ordered that the caciques and their families be exempted from all work because of these responsibilities.[203]

It would seem that the Spaniards were attempting to make the caciques and their families more powerful in the Indian villages than was the aboriginal custom by trying to give them certain limited duties. This amount of control by Indian officers was slight, however, in comparison with that actually exercised by the Spaniards themselves. The authority of the encomendero was, as has been seen, virtually unhampered by the Crown laws which limited his prerogatives in other parts of Spanish America. In addition, the Paraguayan encomendero customarily placed Spanish administrators, called pobleros or mayordomos, in residence in the pueblos to rule the Indians. These men apparently had considerable authority and freedom of action. Ordinances of Ramírez and Hernandarias contain repeated complaints of the pobleros who misused their authority in the villages, keeping Indian girls in concubinage and setting a bad example in general. Alfaro, of course, tried to abolish the use of pobleros altogether, because it conflicted with Crown laws.[204]

It seems likely that at first caciques and their families gradually became more important than under aboriginal conditions, not only because of the few powers and responsibilities placed in their hands by the encomenderos and governors, but also because of the Spanish feudal-like conception of inherited nobility which was extended to include the caciques. For example, Charles V had once decreed that Paraguayan mestizos born of legitimate marriages be regarded as Spaniards and be permitted to hold royal offices because they were descendants of caciques'

[203] Ramírez de Velasco: 1597, ordinances 2, 8, 14, 25; Hernandarias de Saavedra: 1603, ordinance 15.

[204] Ramírez de Velasco: 1597, ordinance 32; Hernandarias de Saavedra: 1603, ordinance 20; Alfaro: 1611, ordinance 13.

families.[205] Thus, it may be considered that the Spanish must have imposed, to some extent, a social class conception upon a society which, aboriginally, was a kinship society with weakly defined status differentiations. It must be added, however, that the administrative power given to Indian officials was limited in the Paraguayan encomienda in comparison with the power which the Crown conceived of as belonging to a proper encomienda organization. As the pobleros and encomenderos, especially the later mestizos, took more unrestricted authority, the status and political importance of caciques probably diminished gradually, in conjunction with the gradual modification of native village social organization.

The encomienda, in general, was a device which prevented close contact of Indians with Spaniards. The Crown desired that, except for religious instruction and protection, the Indians should conduct their own affairs. To this end Spaniards were forbidden access to the villages, and the pueblo government was supposed to be a replica, under Indian officials, of the Spanish town government. Important differences from this conception occurred in Paraguay, however. It has been shown that, except for the cacique and any assistants he may have had, there was no legal provision for Indian officials in the pueblos until Hernandarias desired to create a fiscal in 1603, and Alfaro, in 1611, tried to establish Indian officials after the legal Spanish conception. Meanwhile, Spanish pobleros and mayordomos lived in the Indian villages.[206] These Spanish residents must certainly have had an important voice in pueblo affairs and also served to provide daily examples of customary Spanish behavior. The encomienda towns of Paraguay were not nearly the isolated reservations of Indians cut off from contact with Spanish administrators, or even from day-to-day Spanish life, that the Crown laws provided.

There is no available information with regard to specific innovations or changes which the Spaniards purposely caused, but it may be assumed that some aspects of

[205] Gandía, 1939, p. 58.

[206] Spanish pobleros (or puebleros) were placed in the Indian villages ostensibly to instruct the Indians in politics and law. Fernández: 1618, p. 512.

aboriginal village life were altered in the interests of efficiency of control by the encomenderos or the local administrators. Indian marriages were probably stabilized, and, as was mentioned in Chapter III, the rule that on the death of an Indian the wife and children must continue to live in the husband's house would cause property to be transmitted within the conjugal unit, thus contributing further to the stability of marriages. The extended unilateral kinship groups may have been correspondingly weakened as the Spaniards divided the villages into encomiendas, for it seems inevitable that, because of the small size of many of the encomiendas, large extended kin units would have been divided into separate mita labor groups.

There were also many other disturbances to the village structure. Throughout the years small encomiendas must have been combined occasionally, or growing ones divided. Epidemics may have nearly wiped out some villages, and the further depletion caused by the removal of women by the Spaniards must have been disruptive. All of these occurrences would disturb the delicate balances of house size, population size, subsistence co-operation, and marriage customs, which keep a unilateral kinship unit a smoothly functioning system. Every such disturbance would strengthen the conjugal family pattern at the expense of the consanguineal unit, which was much larger and more complex and thus less able to withstand strains.

Labor and Subsistence

As previously noted, the Spanish Crown laws applying to the New World especially forbade that encomienda Indians be used for any work and stated that a fixed tribute or tax in money or products was the only benefit the encomendero could exact to compensate for his responsibilities. According to Zavala, there is proof that in Mexico and Peru, at least, encomienda labor had come to an end in 1549.[207] Indian labor was secured after 1549 by means of corvée systems called the "quatequil" and the "mita." Corvée labor was not a part of the encomienda system;

[207] Zavala, 1943, pp. 85-86.

conditions of labor were regulated by law, and the Indians were paid on a fixed wage scale.

In Paraguay the mita consisted of labor services required of the encomienda Indians by the Spanish encomendero. It was quite unregulated, and no wages were paid to the Indians. This labor substituted for the tribute which the Indians paid in Mexico and Peru.

Irala's ordinances of 1556, issued when he first granted encomiendas to his followers, state that the Indians were obliged to serve their encomenderos in building houses, in labor, repairs, agricultural work, hunting and fishing, and in any other enterprises, and that they must obey in what they were ordered. The sole restriction placed on the amount of their labor was that only one-fourth of the number of Indians in the encomienda could be used at any one time. This would mean, if complied with, that a given Indian was expected to serve about three months out of the year--assuming work was divided equally among all the Indians. The evidence indicates, however, that this ordinance was not enforced. Irala said nothing about the age limits of the Indians who should work, nor did he forbid the use of women.

Governor Ramírez de Velasco, in 1597, expressly set forth his ordinances to alleviate the hardships of the Indians, because, as he said, "There is no order nor standard for the Indians' work, and the encomendero is served by them with great lack of regulation. . . ." He therefore ordered "that no encomendero should dare to take from his encomienda more than a fourth part, and this means men of 15 to 50 years . . . [but] in time of the harvest of wheat and maize he may take whatever quantity is necessary so long as it is not more than half of them. . . ."

Inasmuch as these ordinances were designed, as stated, to correct abuses, it may be assumed that in Paraguay prior to 1597 the Indians were probably used as a labor force for more than three months of the year, and that women, and children under fifteen, were probably also used at the convenience of the encomendero. This assumption is strengthened by a consideration of Hernandarias' ordinances made six years later.

Hernandarias, like Ramírez, complained of "great lack of regulation in treatment of the Indians," and said that "previous laws had worked more for the advantage of the encomendero than the Indians," thereby implying that the earlier restrictions had been ineffective. His ordinance 5 orders that boys under fifteen, girls under thirteen, and old Indians over sixty be exempt from work. This ordinance is even less restrictive than Ramírez' earlier one, yet Hernandarias felt that he was alleviating hardships of the Indians.

Ordinance 12 directs that no more than one-third of the Indians of a pueblo be taken for the mita, and permits one-half to be taken in the grain and grape harvest. Here again there is evidence of the lack of effectiveness of Ramírez' earlier ordinance. It seems reasonable to judge that inasmuch as Hernandarias was trying to help the Indians, the actual situation must have been quite out of hand, with the Indians sometimes, at least, being forced to work for the encomendero more than four months of the year.

Pedro de Toro, in writing his objections to Alfaro's ordinances, said that the mita had always been for four months of the year "since the cities were founded in Paraguay." De Toro was writing to the Council of the Indies, and it is probable that he did not want to admit that the situation was any worse than that. Inasmuch as he would naturally try to put the encomendero in the best possible light, his statement seems like good evidence that the length of the mita was at least four months of the year.[208]

There has been, so far, no evidence that women did not work in the mita along with the men. One of Hernandarias' ordinances states that should any Indian bring along his wife to cook and care for him during his turn in the mita, the encomendero may not use her for labor. Another forbids women in the mita, except for the wheat harvest, but the general laxity that has been noted makes it seem doubtful whether it was effectively enforced.[209]

One kind of labor that was within the particular province of the Indian women was that of spinning and weaving cloth. Vásquez de Espinosa had noted the aptitude of the

[208] Fernández: 1618, p. 521.

[209] The ordinances referred to in connection with mita labor are: Irala: 1556a, ordinance 5; Ramírez de Velasco: 1597, ordinance 9; Hernandarias de Saavedra: 1603, ordinances 5, 12, 14, 16.

Guaraní for this kind of work in Guayrá,[210] and it is apparent that around Asunción it was an important part of the Indians' labor in the encomiendas. Ramírez' ordinance 42 states: ". . . I am informed that in Indian pueblos, where they make cloth, that after the Indian women are each given four ounces of cotton to spin for the four days of the week they are to work, some of them are not able to finish their task and must work all the week. I do not blame the encomendero for this. . . ." In another context, Ramírez described this work of the women as follows: "The tax that they have today is that they work four days a week spinning a little cotton or wool. For each day, every Indian woman is given three ounces of cotton, and they return one of thread . . . they do this for ten months, because the other two are for work in their own fields. They work, not counting fiesta days, 136 days; so that each woman spins 8 1/2 pounds of thread a year, and 70 yards of cloth of 20 to 22 pounds, which are worth 30 pesos to 8 reales. . . ."[211]

In regions where the yerba mate grew wild, Indians were intensively employed in the labor of cutting, curing, and carrying it to market. The yerba was one of the first of the few cash crops ever to be developed in Paraguay, and by the beginning of the seventeenth century the residents of Villarrica and Ciudad Real were engaged in its preparation and commerce.[212] Ruiz de Montoya, who wrote of the early years of the seventeenth century, mentioned the lack of any kind of money in Paraguay, and noted that the yerba mate served as the principal medium of exchange.[213]

Apparently, the amount of labor expended in collecting the yerba and transporting it to Asunción and Santa Fé was very great, for article 31 of Alfaro's revised ordinances forbids the Indians to collect it even of their own free will in certain times of the year.[214] Hernandarias, writing to the King in 1617, referred to an order of his own which would stop the "incredible labor . . . and great

[210] Vásquez de Espinosa, 1942, p. 687.

[211] Ramírez de Velasco, quoted in Gandía, 1939, p. 89.

[212] R. I. Cardozo, 1938b, p. 79.

[213] Ruiz de Montoya, 1892, pp. 16-17.

[214] Consejo de Indias: 1618.

harm" which the work connected with the yerba caused.[215]

The transportation of products from the farms to the city markets was another kind of labor for which the Indians were used. Ramírez de Velasco's article 19 specifies that "no one shall order any Indian man or woman to bear burdens, as there are many cheap horses and an abundance of carts--except in the interior where there are so many swamps where horses and carts cannot go. In these places, Indians may be used provided they are paid in useful articles such as farm implements or clothing . . . ." Alfaro's article 33, written in 1611, fourteen years after Ramírez issued his ordinances, again requires that Indians shall not be used as carriers, and number 30 requires that mita Indians be used to carry only water and wood. In response to this order Pedro de Toro declared that this was impossible to fulfill in Guayrá, where there were no other means of transport.[216]

The two rivers bordering Paraguay provided an important means of transportation, and Indians were used to row boats and pole rafts which carried cargoes between towns. Ruiz de Montoya mentioned that "large boats go up and down carrying agricultural produce, the most ordinary being sugar, honey, wine, wax, hemp, and the yerba. . . ." [217] Alfaro's ordinances of 1611, which were designed to abolish servitude and substitute wage labor, state in article 26, that "mita Indians . . . who row up and down the river [should be paid] four pesos in four yards of woolen or cotton cloth." [218]

It was customary for travelers, soldiers, and merchants to take Indians with them on their journeys, probably to aid in the various labors involved in travel, and possibly also for protection. Ramírez' ordinance 21 would prevent "citizens, soldiers, and merchants from taking Indians out of the state without a license from the Justicia Mayor of the city from which they were leaving . . . and the Indians would be paid in clothing or the skins that are used here for clothing . . . as it has been customary to give them nothing of value. . . ." Hernandarias' ordinance

[215] Hernandarias: 1617, p. 506.

[216] Fernández: 1618, p. 519.

[217] Ruiz de Montoya, 1892, p. 16.

[218] Alfaro: 1611.

21 makes a similar ruling "because there is great lawlessness. . . ." The Council of the Indies, in modifying Alfaro's ordinances, provided in article 18 that: "When merchants or anyone who has business in the province have to travel from one part of the province to another and need Indians for the trip, they may not take them, even though the Indians may wish to go, without written permission of the Governor. . . ."

These repeated rulings that travelers must register, or receive permission to use Indians, were necessary because very often the Indians did not return to their own encomiendas. As Ramírez put it in his above-cited ordinance, ". . . this has caused a great diminution of Indians in this province. . . ." There had to be "legal security that the Indians be returned in the designated time. . . ."[219]

The mita labor on Spanish farms was of considerable importance when contrasted with the possibilities of acculturation had the Indians paid only a yearly tribute. In Paraguay the Indian laborers worked closely under the supervision of the encomendero or his administrators and thus learned Spanish agricultural techniques and the cultivation of European crops. The Spaniards, too, were in a favorable position to avail themselves of useful aboriginal foods and techniques.

Various crops were grown on the Spanish farms, some native, some introduced by the Spaniards. Jaime Rasquín, in 1558, listed grapes, sugar cane, figs, pomegranates, oranges, and citrons as having been introduced from Spain.[220] Manuel de Frías mentioned hemp, flax, ginger, almonds, maize, wheat, and barley.[221]

Captain Martín de Orue described the products of Paraguay quite fully in his letter to the King in 1573:

"This city [Asunción] and its land provides a great deal of food in such a way that nearly all the year harvests are made from the farms, because the maize gives

[219]The ordinances mentioned above are from Ramírez de Velasco: 1597; Hernandarias: 1603; Alfaro: 1611; Consejo de Indias: 1618.

[220]" . . . ay muchas plantas despenya huvas asucar higueras granados naranjos sidras," Gondra MS 478b.

[221]" . . . ay canamo y lino xengibre almendras maiz trigo cevada," Gondra MS 32c.

two crops a year every six months and each harvest lasts three months. . . . In one-half of the year they harvest maize, kidney beans, horse beans [or broad beans], gourds, melons, mandulgues, grapes, figs, pomegranates, and cotton. They make wine which this year is more than 6,000 arrobas [4.26 gallons of wine per arroba], and which is growing in importance. . . . In the other half year they harvest maize, cotton, potatoes, oats, and manioc, which is a fine food . . . which they eat all the year . . . and kidney beans which they call 'tupis' . . . and sugar cane. . . .

"There is a great deal of fishing in this river, and hunting of deer, partridges, pigeons, and turtledoves. . . .

"There are very beautiful pastures for the cattle and horses that the people use. One league below the city there are some very good salt pans . . . [near the city] there is saltpeter to make powder . . . on this side of the river are the best and most beautiful pastures, agricultural fields and springs in the world.

"There are many herds of cattle, goats, sheep, horses, and pigs. . . . The only things lacking for human sustenance are iron, metals, and olive oil . . . and some priests, because those there are so few, and almost all are old and sick."[222]

Father Ruiz de Montoya related that the wheat was very good, but that they grew only enough for the sacrament and a few gifts, as everyone ate manioc instead. He also mentioned that wax was made from the honeycombs of wild bees.[223]

The Spanish introductions which were probably of greatest utility to the Indians were the domestic animals, as aboriginally all meat had been obtained from hunting. According to evidence in Irala's ordinance 9,[224] chicken and pork became part of the Indians' subsistence at an early date. Some cattle, goats, sheep, and horses probably later became part of the economy of the Indian pueblos, as the Indians had ample opportunity to learn the techniques of caring for these animals. Hunting and fishing were not entirely given up, but probably diminished in importance as these new sources of food became more

[222] Orue: 1573, pp. 163-64.

[223] Ruiz de Montoya, 1892, p. 17.

[224] Irala: 1556a.

plentiful. Inasmuch as herding was learned from the Spaniards, it was probably entirely a male activity, and insofar as it tended to supplant the traditional male activity of hunting, it must have had cultural effects beyond the fact of increased subsistence.

The acquisition of domestic animals probably did not require the planting of cattle feed such as alfalfa, since there were large areas of excellent pasturage available all the year. Also, because of the abundance of pasturage, herding did not crowd the Indians from their best agricultural lands as it did in Peru.

European garden vegetables did not find favor in Paraguay, and although the country was well suited to rice, it was not adopted in the early colonial period. Wine and wheat were necessary for the sacrament; wine may have become of some daily importance, but wheat never competed with the better adapted maize and manioc.

Sugar cane and citrus fruits were two introduced crops which were especially favored by the Paraguayan climate. The yerba mate was an indigenous plant, but after the arrival of the Spaniards, the custom of brewing a tea from its leaves grew in importance and it soon was in common use among both Spaniards and Indians.

There is no evidence that any of the crops of European provenience were not used by the Indians, nor that any indigenous crops were not favored by the Spaniards. In the earliest days the Spaniards probably depended somewhat on wheat as a staple, as it is often mentioned by the chroniclers, but later generations used manioc instead.[225] Apparently, the mixture of Spanish and Indian subsistence was quite complete.

Religious Instruction

According to Azara, only one cleric came to Paraguay with the conquerors. Twenty years later the first bishop and some other clerics arrived, making a total of seventeen, but only one of them knew the Guaraní language, and he did not know it well enough to translate the catechism. Later, after new Spanish towns and forty Indian pueblos

[225]Ruiz de Montoya, 1892, p. 17.

had been founded, there were twenty ecclesiastics, of which only two knew Guaraní well enough to try to proselytize the Indians.[226]

Francisco de Alfaro, who, as a representative of the Crown, had had opportunity to visit other colonies, informed the King in 1611 that Paraguay, even more than Tucumán, had a great lack of ecclesiastics, and that since Paraguay was such an isolated land, the need there was even greater.[227] According to Adrián Cornejo, writing to the King as late as 1660, lenten restrictions were not observed and "Indians as well as Spaniards eat meat with no distinction of one day from another, a most scandalous thing. . . ."[228]

Pedro Diego de Torres, writing in 1609, said: ". . . very few Christian Indians have any information about our Lord, and many have none, and in some places there are infidel Indians that have served the Spaniards for many years already without the Spaniards caring if they become Christians. . . ."[229] The same Jesuit, writing in 1614, spoke "of a town of Indians called Guarambaré, not very far from the city [Asunción], which has been deprived of all spiritual assistance for 15 years, [a town] most poor, composed of already Christianized Indians, who serve the Spaniards of the city."[230] This seems a rather significant commentary on lack of religious instruction in Paraguay, because this was a large pueblo not far from Asunción.

Statements by Ramírez de Velasco and Hernandarias have been quoted which show that the Indians were often kept at work on Sundays and fiesta days, and reference has been made to ordinances which required caciques' sons

[226] Azara, 1040, p. 170.

[227] Alfaro: 1611-12, pp. 449-50.

[228] "Tambien he hallado que con una necessidad fantastica de que no ay mantenimientos de quaresma generalmente en ella y los demas dias de ayuno se comia carne assi por los indios como por los espanoles sin que hubiesse distinssion de dias a dias cossa que me ha paressido escandalossissima y de mal exemplo para los indios he puesto el hombro a que se quite abuso tan malo y jusgo lo consequire por vencerlos con rasson que no ay necessidad que a esto obligue ni que pueda honestar acssion tal." Gondra MS 278.

[229] Cartas Anuas, 1927-29, 19:13.

[230] Ibid., p. 273.

to recite the prayers and teach other Indians. Hernandarias' article 2 was an order that churches be built, article 3, that encomenderos give religious instruction, and article 8 required that an Indian fiscal be appointed who would be in charge of indoctrination. Whether or not these ordinances were ever carried out, it is evident that if there were to be much indoctrination of the Indians, it would be done by the encomendero and by the already indoctrinated Indians.[231]

Had there been the necessary religious personnel, it seems likely that the conversion of the Guaraní would not have been difficult, to judge from the experience of the extraordinarily successful Jesuit missionaries in Guayrá. The Guaraní did not have large communities with great public rites and ceremonies managed by a hierarchy of priests who would fight against all change. No great campaigns against "idolatry," such as occurred in Peru in the early seventeenth century, would have been necessary in Paraguay. The small Guaraní communities and their simple socioreligious structure would probably not have resisted acculturation in this any more than they did in other aspects of their culture.

But it seems clear from the evidence that the encomienda Indians of Paraguay were not converted to Christianity as rapidly or as thoroughly as in other Spanish-American regions, even though their acculturation in other aspects of life was more complete. In Mexico and Peru, for example, the rigid encomiendas and legal restrictions retarded assimilation of the Indians into the colonial way of life in every respect except in the sphere of religion. The encomiendas were purposely organized to further religious conversion of the natives, and the ecclesiastics were, at the same time, fervent upholders of the Crown restrictions against the contact of lay Spaniards with the Indian pueblos. In Paraguay the smaller numbers of ecclesiastics and their consequent lack of political power made their outcries against the violations of Crown orders relatively ineffectual, so that they were unable to prevent Spanish-Guaraní secular relations from being close. Meanwhile, the religious conversion of the Indians lagged.

[231] Ramírez de Velasco: 1597; Hernandarias: 1603.

VI. CONCLUSIONS

In general, the outstanding difference between the colonization of Paraguay and that of better-known regions in Spanish America was the rapidity and thoroughness with which the aborigines were adapted to Spanish culture in Paraguay and integrated into a self-sufficient colony which developed national characteristics very early in its history. The conclusion seems inescapable that Guaraní culture was so quickly altered because of the special structure of the encomiendas, which actually fostered, rather than retarded, the assimilation of the Indians into the dominant Spanish culture patterns. This unusual effect of the encomiendas in Paraguay, for its part, was a product of purely local circumstances which were quite different from the conditions in Mexico, Central America, and Peru.

The culture of the Guaraní differed considerably from the aboriginal cultures the Spaniards encountered in Mexico and Peru. The society was not politically unified nor class structured,[232] and the villages were small and only semipermanent. This meant that the Spaniards could not simply place themselves in the position of the top-level native rulers for purposes of control and exploitation through subsidiary chiefs. The Indian pueblos had to be reduced to permanency and eventually to be made larger than the simple kinship units which had composed the aboriginal villages. These adjustments also necessitated personalized control by the Spaniards, which was obtained by pobleros who lived in the new Indian villages and enforced the fundamental changes which were to disrupt Guaraní society.

Another circumstance which affected the relationship between Spaniards and Guaraní was the isolation of Paraguay from the normal currents of trade with the other colonies and with Spain. The absence of mineral resources or other important marketable wealth contributed to the commercial isolation, and the people were reduced

[232]Recent studies by Kubler, 1946, and Gibson, 1948, give good accounts of the importance of the Inca political and class structure in determining the nature of the political controls used by the Spaniards in Peru. These provide a most effective contrast to the Paraguayan situation.

to a barter economy. This had important consequences for the encomienda system, since there was no exportable product of sufficient value to be used as tribute from the encomienda Indians. These factors also prevented the development of a large trading class and thus inhibited the spread of middle-class attitudes, so that the gulf between the ideology of a money economy and that of the Indian production-for-use economy was never as great in Paraguay as in most of Latin America.

Even the influence of the Church was unusual in Paraguay. In most of the important areas of Spanish America the clergy usually exerted its strength against the exploitation of natives by lay Spaniards and was important in aiding the enforcement of the Crown policy of segregation of encomienda Indians from Spanish colonists. Clerical influence in central Paraguay, however, was relatively unimportant; there the Spaniards, and later the irreligious mestizos, completed the secular acculturation of the Guaraní with little opposition from the powerless clergy, the reverse of the trend observed in Mexico and Peru.

Since the country was unattractive to Spanish colonists, peninsular Spaniards were soon in such a minority that the ruling population was predominantly mestizo, and the remaining Indians were then subjected to a dominant culture which was somewhat different from the original Spanish. As race mixture increased, the number of encomienda Indians diminished. Such demographic factors contributed indirectly to a more rapid Indian acculturation, for as the encomiendas became smaller, control by individual encomenderos became more direct and personal. The small size of the encomiendas was also an important reason why tribute could not be substituted for labor; there were too few Indians to supply anything but the barest subsistence.

These local circumstances so altered the two Paraguayan institutions for control of the aborigines, the originario and mitayo encomiendas, that the ruling population and the Indians were brought into close relationship. The originario system was especially noteworthy in this respect, for the Indians were so completely under the domination of individual Spaniards that their acculturation must have been rapid and thorough. In the mitayo encomienda kinship ties between the encomendero and his Indians were possibly less pervasive, but the nature of the labor services and the fact that representatives of Spanish culture lived in the Indian towns brought the Guaraní and Spaniards into a much closer community than would have been possible under a more ideal Spanish encomienda.

The originario Indians worked permanently on the lands of the Spaniards. Guaraní women, many of whom were wives or concubines of the encomenderos, constituted a large proportion of these Indians; others were relatives of these women. Relationship ties of both consanguinity and affinity became an important aspect of the association of the encomendero with his workers, for aboriginal customs such as status polygyny, the role of women as agricultural workers, and kinship labor obligations were by this means incorporated into the colonial system. The close and permanent association of the originario Indians with their Spanish masters also resulted in the merging of native and introduced traits in such things as food and food preparation and agricultural methods. As the mestizo descendants of the originario polygyny became the basic "Spanish" population, perhaps a few other habits and customs may have been derived directly from association with their Guaraní mothers and relatives. The retention of the Guaraní language is an obvious example of this sort of cultural survival.

The position of these mestizos in Paraguayan affairs after about 1580 is, from the standpoint of Indian acculturation, one of the most significant of the several unusual characteristics of the colony. The large population of somewhat bicultural mixed bloods succeeded true Spaniards in positions of authority as political officials and encomenderos. Thus, ties of kinship between encomenderos and Indians became stronger, linguistic barriers ceased to exist, and, in general, cultural and racial differences between the two classes of society were lessened. The Indians probably had considerably more affinity for a feudal-like noncommercial society, the members of which spoke Guaraní and possessed a comprehension of Guaraní culture.

The mitayo Indians, although in the early years they were more numerous than the originarios, did not figure so importantly as contributors to the developing Paraguayan culture, but they were profoundly affected by the dominant culture in ways which were implicit in the form of the mitayo encomienda, and they were thus rapidly incorporated into the national life.

The mitayo Indians paid no tribute, but were used as an unpaid, part-time labor force on the lands of the encomendero, serving about one-third of a year or more. The rest of the year they lived in their own villages. Since, in the absence of political unification in the native society, the Spaniards could not govern indirectly through native rulers, it was necessary that these villages be ruled by the encomenderos or by Spanish administrators who lived in them. Kinship ties, similar to those of the originario, were a part of the means of control, as the encomendero often took Indian women from the towns to augment the numbers of his originarios.[233] The Spanish pobleros of the Indian villages also had Indian concubines, and thus were related affinally to many of the village Indians. The small size of the encomiendas was also important in permitting Spanish control to be complete and personal, reaching down to the individual Indian.

The mitayo encomienda altered Guaraní village life in many ways. Villages were made larger and more permanent, and the aboriginal sociopolitical organization was quickly displaced by Spanish internal rule as the various powers of the native chiefs were taken over by encomenderos and pobleros. Indian marriages were stabilized, and the extended family or lineage unit was correspondingly weakened. The general influence of the mitayo system modified the aboriginal village and kinship structure toward a Spanish type of town with emphasis on the conjugal family unit.

Many Spanish cultural elements were simply added to the native inventory. The unspecialized labor for four or more months of the year under the direction of the encomenderos led to a knowledge of animal husbandry and new skills in agriculture. As native and introduced subsistence items merged in Paraguayan economy, so they probably did in the mitayo pueblos, although perhaps not so rapidly. The various European domestic animals were

[233]Díaz de Guzmán, who was in Paraguay in the early seventeenth century, said that the encomienda Indians were called "Tobayá," which means "in-law relative." 1943, p. 110.

of greatest value to the Indians, as they filled an important gap in the native economy. Improved tools and weapons and transportation by wheeled vehicles, horses, burros, and oxen, together with the more efficient food economy, permitted much larger population aggregates.

One of the important consequences of the rather unusual form of the colonization of Paraguay was that the few Spaniards, the many mestizos, and the acculturated Indians came to form a true, culturally independent nation with distinctive institutions much earlier than most of the other areas of South America. Although the early Spanish rulers had added such elements of nationhood as political, economic, military, and religious institutions rather than replaced them, as in Peru and Mexico, the unusual form of the encomienda rapidly introduced the bulk of the aboriginal population into colonial life, with the consequent local pride in national language, territory, and customs. The "comunero" revolts which presaged the national wars of independence in most of Spanish America had their inception in revolts by Paraguayan mestizos before the colony was fifty years old,[234] and subsequent revolts against Spanish authority characterized most of the remaining colonial period in Paraguay. In other South American countries many of the important national movements did not take place until the eighteenth century.

The isolation of the early conquistadores from political and commercial ties with Spain left the colony virtually self-ruled from the beginning. The military alliance with the Guaraní and the economic dependence on the "harems" of Guaraní women gave the Indians an important role in the life of the colony, for the Spaniards desperately needed their help during the early years. The nearly continuous wars and expeditions made complete military control of the Guaraní necessary and also tended to make the tribe an integral part of the colony almost from the first year of the contact. The small number of Spaniards in the colony and its subsequent rapid diminution left mestizos and acculturated Guaraní Indians as the dominant groups in all classes of the society.

[234]In a sense, the successful revolt against the Crown's governor, Cabeza de Vaca, by the followers of Irala was a "national" or "comunero" movement as early as 1545!

It would seem that the type of acculturation which occurred in Paraguay must have resulted in the replacement of much of Guaraní culture, with the exception of the language, the role of women, certain food crops and cookery, and perhaps a few miscellaneous items of folklore and superstition. As has happened with the beginnings of national consciousness in most of the countries of the world, pride of language or dialect became greatly exalted. The heavy preponderance of Guaraní-speaking mestizos naturally resulted in the preference for the Guaraní language over the Spanish under the circumstances of the feeling against Spain. The continuation and perhaps accentuation of the intense nationalism since the devastation caused by the War of the Triple Alliance in the 1870's has kept Guaraní in use as a national language to this day, in an atmosphere similar to what has been called "revivalism" or "nativism" in more primitive societies. Probably most other elements of true Guaraní culture have long since been lost. It would seem that, although Spanish-Indian racial and cultural mixture took place to some extent in all of Spanish America, two general trends were unusual in Paraguay--the rapid loss of Indian social and cultural integrity, and the retention of the language due to the same rapid amalgamation of the Indians into a colonial society which developed national characteristics at a very early date in its history.

SELECTED BIBLIOGRAPHY

Acarete du Biscay, 1698. An Account of a Voyage Up the River de la Plata, and Thence Over Land to Peru. With Observations on the Inhabitants, as well Indians and Spaniards; the Cities, Commerce, Fertility, and Riches of That Part of America. London: Buckley.

Acosta, Gregorio de: 1545. Relación breve en el Río de la Plata fecha por Gregorio de Acosta para su magestad e para su real Consejo de Indias. In Garay, 1899-1901, 1:10-18.

Alfaro, Francisco de: 1611. Ordenanzas de Alfaro. In Hernández, 1913, 2:661-77, Appendix No. 56. Condensed in Gandía, 1939, pp. 435-42, Appendix No. XX.

_____: 1611-12. Cinco cartas de Don Francisco de Alfaro en que se dan cuenta a S. M. de su visita en el Tucuman, y sobre otros varios asuntos, Santiago del Estero, 22 y 24 de diciembre de 1611, y 20 de enero de 1612. In Gandía, 1939, pp. 446-51, Appendix, Document XXII.

Angelís, Pedro de, 1836-37. Colección de obras y documentos relativos á la historia antigua y moderna de las provincias del Río de la Plata. Buenos Aires: Imprenta del Estado. 6 vols.

Anonymous: 1545. Relación del Río de la Plata. In Garay, 1899-1901, 1:43-51.

Aviles, Marqués de: 1800. Copia del informe que hizo a S. M. el Exmo. Señor Marqués de Aviles siendo Virrey de Buenos Ayres sobre el gobierno temporal y espiritual pasado y presente de los treinta pueblos de las misiones Guaranís en complimiento de repetidas r. ordenes a cuyo tenor has sido librada la R[1]. Cédula de 17 de mayo de 1803, que dispone la variación de dho. gobierno. In Lastarría, 1914, pp. 26-53.

Azara, Félix de, 1923. Viajes por la América meridional. Madrid: Calpe. 2 vols.

_____, 1943. Descripción e historia del Paraguay y del Río de la Plata. Buenos Aires: Editorial Bajel.

Báez, Cicilio, 1926. Historia colonial del Paraguay y Río de la Plata. Asunción: Zamphirópolos.

Barber, Ruth Kerns, 1932. Indian Labor in the Spanish Colonies. Albuquerque: Univ. New Mexico Press.

Benedict, Ruth, 1936. Marital Property Rights in Bilateral Society. Amer. Anthropol., 38:368-73.

Cabeza de Vaca, Alvar Núñez: 1542. Estatutos y ordenanzas que mandó publicar el gobernador D. Alvar Núñez Cabeza de Vaca, sobre el trato y gobierno de los indios. 5 de abril. In García Santillán, 1928, pp. 347-56, Appendix.

Cardozo, Efraim, 1938. Las Ordenanzas de Montejo. Congreso internacional de historia de América II°. Buenos Aires. 2:121-27.

Cardozo, Ramón I., 1938a. Villa Rica del Espíritu Santo, o el éxodo de un pueblo. Congreso internacional de historia de América II°. Buenos Aires. 2:128-41.

_____, 1938b. La Antigua provincia de Guairá y la Villa Rica del Espíritu Santo. Buenos Aires: J. Menéndez.

Cartas anuas de la provincia del Paraguay, Chile y Tucumán, de la Compañía de Jesús, 1927-29, Documentos para la historia argentina. Buenos Aires: Iglesia. Vols. 19-20.

Cartas de Indias, 1877. Madrid: M. G. Hernández. 2 vols.

Cédula Real: 1679. Redúzcanse los indios originarios a mitayos, y júntense como los demás en pueblos. In Hernández, 1913, 2:688-90, Appendix No. 61.

Cepeda: 1591. Carta a S. M. del licenciado Cepeda . . . La Plata, 15 de marzo. In Levillier, 1922, 3:110-17.

Consejo de Indias: 1618. Decisión real en el Consejo de Indias, aprobatoria de las ordenanzas de Alfaro, con las modificaciones en ellas introducidas. In Hernández, 1913, 2:677-81, Appendix No. 57. Condensed in Gandía, 1939, pp. 442-45, Appendix No. XXI.

Díaz de Guzmán, Ruy, 1943. La Argentina. Buenos Aires: A. Estrada.

Dobrizhoffer, Martin, 1822. An Account of the Abipones, an Equestrian People of Paraguay. London: J. Murray. 3 vols.

Dorantes, Pedro: n.d. Parecer que dió el factor [Pedro Dorantes] de lo que se devía hazer en la entrada del Paraguay. In Garay, 1899-1901, 1:128-31.

_____: 1545. Carta del factor Pedro de Orantes, al rey, sobre la necesidad de dar a los indios un trato distinto del que reciben, y la conveniencia de dividir la provincia en dos gobernaciones separadas por el Paraná e Río Ipatí. La Asumpción, 5 de marzo. In Levillier, 1915, 1:80-82.

_____: 1553. Requerimiento del factor Dorantes para que poblase y encomendase indios y su respuesta por el teniente de gobernador Irala. In Lafuente Machain, 1939, pp. 483-90, Appendix. Also in García Santillán, 1928, Appendix, pp. 403-9.

_____: 1573. Carta de Pedro Dorantes al Consejo de Indias. Asunción, 8 de abril. In Garay, 1899-1901, 1:131-47.

Fernández, Bartólome, and Pedro de Toro: 1618. Alegatos presentados, en grado de apelación, ante el Consejo de Indias, por Bartólome Fernandez y Pedro de Toro, produrador general de las provincias del Paraguay, acerca de la revocación y anulación de varios artículos de las ordenanzas de Don Francisco de Alfaro. In Gandía, 1939, pp. 510-23, Appendix, Document XLII.

Gandía, Enrique de, 1932a. Los Primeros italianos en el Río de la Plata y otros estudios históricos. Buenos Aires: García Santos.

_____, 1932b. Indios y conquistadores en el Paraguay. Buenos Aires: García Santos.

_____, 1932c. Historia de la conquista del Río de la Plata y del Paraguay. Buenos Aires: García Santos.

_____, 1939. Francisco de Alfaro y la condición social de los indios. Buenos Aires: "El Ateneo."

Garay, Blas, 1895. Pequeña biblioteca histórica. Asunción: H. Kraus.

_____, 1899-1901. Colección de documentos relativos á la historia de América y particularmente á la historia del Paraguay. Asunción: H. Kraus.

_____, 1942. Tres ensayos sobre historia del Paraguay. Asunción: Editorial Guaranía.

García Santillán, Juán Carlos, 1928. Legislación sobre indios del Río de la Plata en el siglo XVI. Madrid: Imprenta del Asilo de Huérfanos del S. C. de Jesús.

Gibson, Charles, 1948. The Inca Concept of Sovereignty and the Spanish Administration in Peru. Latin-American Studies, IV. Univ. Texas Instit. Latin-American Studies.

Gondra, Manuel E., MSS Collection. Univ. Texas Library.

32c. Frías, Manuel de. Semillas introducidas en las provincias del Río de la Plata y Paraguay. Buenos Aires, May 21, 1621.

38a. Frías, Manuel de. Solicitud de Frías . . . sobre la necesidad de introducir negros africanos para los trabajos de la colonia. Buenos Aires (?), 1617 (?).

209a. León, Sebastián de. Carta a S. M. sobre la pobreza de los españoles en el Paraguay. Asunción, September 7, 1639.

209c. Información al procurador general sobre la pobreza de los vecinos del Paraguay, hecha por los padres religiosos. Asunción, April 3, 1643.

209d. Petición ante el teniente general del Paraguay que se sirva suspender la media anata en la dicha provincia. Asunción, March 3, 1640.

278. Cornejo, Adrián. Carta a S. M. dando cuenta de una visita a los dominios del obispado. Villa Rica del Espíritu Santo, August 20, 1660.

478b. Rasquín, Jaime. Carta de Jayme Rasquín a S. C. R. Mag[d]. 1558 (?).

515i. Felipe II. Asiento y capitulación con el capitán Juán Ortiz de Çarate sobre la conquista y población de las provincias del Río de la Plata. Madrid, July 10, 1579.

515j. Felipe II. Instrucción de lo quel adelantado Juán Ortiz de Çarate a de guardar en la población del Río de la Plata. Aranjuez, May 16, 1571.

725ℓ. Téllez de Escobar, Diego. Relación de las cosas que han pasado en la provincia del Río de la Plata, desde que prendieron al governador Cabeza de Vaca. 1556 (?).

1036. Reje Gorvalán, Felipe. Carta a S. M. sobre el estado de la provincia del Paraguay. Asunción, October 20, 1677.

1436. Villa Rica del Espíritu Santo, Cabildo de. Carta representando la imposibilidad de aplicar las ordenanzas de Alfaro. Villa Rica, March 26, 1612.

1442. Asunción, Cabildo de. Carta a S. M. sobre cosas tocantes al buen gobierno de las provincias del Río de la Plata y Paraguay. April 20, 1612.

2030. Torre, Manuel Antonio de la. Razón que de su visita general da el Dr. D. Manuel Ant° Delatorre, obispo del Paraguay al real y supremo Consejo de Indias en 1761. Asunción, September 28, 1761.

Gonzales, Martín: 1556. Carta de Martín Gonzales, clérigo, al emperador Don Carlos, dando noticia de las expediciones hechas y de los atropellos cometidos después de la prisión del gobernador Alvar Núñez Cabeza de Vaca. Asunción, 25 de junio. In Cartas de Indias, 1877, 1:604-18, Document CIII.

Guevara, Isabel de: 1556. Carta de Doña Isabel de Guevara a la Princesa Doña Juana. Asunción, 2 de julio. In Garay, 1895, pp. 94-97. Also in Cartas de Indias, 1877, 1:619-21, Document CIV.

Guevara, José, 1836. Historia del Paraguay, Río de la Plata y Tucumán. In Angelís, 1836-37, Vol. II.

Gunther, John, 1941. Inside Latin America. New York: Harper and Brothers.

Haggard, J. Villasana, and Malcolm Dallas McLean, 1941. Handbook for Translators of Spanish Historical Documents. Austin: Univ. Texas Press.

Hanke, Lewis, 1935. The First Social Experiments in America; a Study in the Development of Spanish Indian Policy in the Sixteenth Century. Cambridge: Harvard Univ. Press.

Haring, Clarence Henry, 1918. Trade and Navigation Between Spain and the Indies in the Time of the Hapsburgs. Cambridge: Harvard Univ. Press.

Hernandarias de Saavedra: 1603. Ordenanzas dadas por el gobernador y capitán general justicia mayor, y juez de residencia de las provincias del Río de la Plata Don Hernan Arias de Saavedra, sobre el tratamiento de los indios, 29 de diciembre. In García Santillán, 1928, pp. 376-88. Also in Gandía, 1939, pp. 346-63, Appendix, Document VI.

_____: 1617. Carta del gobernador del Río de la Plata, Arias de Saavedra, en que refiere a S. M. el aumento de reducciónes de indios en aquellas provincias desde que fué nombrado gobernador, y que por falta de obispo no había dado el resultado que se esperaba; sobre las iglesias que había construido, y que podría evitarse la venida de religiosos de España por haberlos en el país, y que ha hecho guardar las ordenanzas de Don Francisco de Alfaro, acerca del uso de la yerba, de la tasa y servicio personal de los indios, de la matanza del ganado, etc.—acompaña algunos testimonios en prueba de lo referido. Buenos Aires, 8 de julio. In Gandía, 1939, pp. 504-10, Appendix, Document XLI.

Hernández, Pablo, 1913. Organización social de las doctrinas guaraníes de la Compañía de Jesús. Barcelona: Gili. 2 vols.

Herrera y Tordesillas, Antonio de, 1934. Historia general de los hechos de los castellanos en las islas y tierrafirme del mar océano. Madrid: Academia de la Historia. Vol. I.

Irala, Domingo Martínez de: 1541-47. Ordenanzas. In Lafuente Machain, 1939, pp. 415-35, Appendix.

_____: 1556a. Ordenanzas sobre repartimientos y encomiendas —14 de mayo. In Lafuente Machain, 1939, pp. 511-24, Appendix.

_____: 1556b. Relación breve con parecer de Domingo de Irala, gobernador de la provincia del Río de la Plata, por su magestad para el ilustrisimo señor Marqués de Mondejar del Consejo de las Indias. In Lafuente Machain, 1939, pp. 535-46, Appendix.

_____: 1556c. Testamento—13 de marzo. In Lafuente Machain, 1939, pp. 547-65, Appendix.

James, Preston E., 1942. Latin America. New York: Odyssey Press.

Kirkpatrick, F. A., 1939. Latin America. New York: Macmillan Co.

_____, 1942. The Landless Encomienda. Hispanic Amer. Hist. Rev., 22:765-74.

Kubler, George, 1946. The Quechua in the Colonial World. In Steward (ed.), 1946-50, 2:331-410.

La Farge, Oliver, 1940. Maya Ethnology: The Sequence of Cultures. In: The Maya and Their Neighbors. New York: Appleton-Century. Pp. 281-91.

Lafuente Machain, R. de, 1939. El Gobernador Domingo Martínez de Irala. Buenos Aires: Bernabé y cía.

Lamas, Andrés, (ed.), 1849. Colección de memorias y documentos para la historia y jeografía de los pueblos del Río de la Plata. Montevideo.

Las Casas, Bartólome de, 1909. Apologética historia de las Indias. Madrid: Bailly, Bailliére e hijos.

Lastarría, Miguel, 1914. Colonias orientales del Río Paraguay ó de la Plata. Buenos Aires: Compañía sud-americana de billetes de banco.

León Pinelo, Antonio de, 1922. Tratado de las confirmaciones reales. Buenos Aires: J. Peuser.

_____, 1943. El Paraíso en el Nuevo Mundo. Lima: Torres Aguirre. 2 vols.

Levene, Ricardo, 1937. A History of Argentina. Chapel Hill: Univ. North Carolina Press.

Levillier, Roberto (ed), 1915. Correspondencia de los oficiales reales de hacienda del Río de la Plata con los reyes de España. Madrid: "Sucesores de Rivadeneyra."

_____, 1915-18. Correspondencia de la ciudad de Buenos Aires con los reyes de España; documentos del archivo de Indias. Madrid: n. publ. 3 vols.

_____, 1918-22. La Audiencia de Charcas. Correspondencia de presidentes y oidores, documentos del archivo de Indias. Madrid: J. Pueyo. 3 vols.

López de Velasco, Juán, 1894. Geografía y descripción universal de las Indias. Madrid: Fortanet.

Lujan de Medina, Jerónimo: 1612. Certificación dada en forma de capítulos por Fray Jerónimo Lujan de Medina, vicario provincial de la orden de la merced, y por varios religiosos de la misma, en que hacen constar los males que resultarían de establecerse en el Paraguay la tasa entre los indios naturales, según lo mandado en las ordenanzas de Don Francisco de Alfaro. Asunción, 19 marzo. In Gandía, 1939, pp. 453-61. Appendix, Document XXIV.

Métraux, Alfred, 1948. The Guaraní. In Steward (ed.), 1946-50, 3:69-94.

Mitre, Bartólome, 1887. Historia de Belgrano y de la independencia argentina. Buenos Aires: F. Lajouane. 3 vols.

Montalvo, Hernando de: 1579. Carta de Hernando de Montalvo, tesorero del Río de la Plata, dando cuenta a S. M. de los sucesos y estado de aquellas provincias. Asunción. 15 de noviembre. In Peña, 1935, pp. 102-20. Also in Levillier, 1915, pp. 321-41.

______: 1585. Carta del tesorero Hernando de Montalvo a Su Magestad. Buenos Aires, 12 de octubre. In Peña, 1935, pp. 129-45. Also in Levillier, 1915, pp. 361-87.

Moreno, Fulgencio R., 1926. La Ciudad de la Asunción. Buenos Aires: J. Suárez.

Moses, Bernard, 1898. The Establishment of Spanish Rule in America. New York: G. P. Putnam's Sons.

Ortiz de Vergara, Francisco: 1569. Memorias de Francisco Ortiz de Vergara dadas a su merced el señor visitador. In Garay, 1899-1901, 1:97-99.

Orue, Martín de: 1573. Carta del capitán Martín de Orue para S. M. Asumpción, 14 de abril. In Garay, 1899-1901, 1:159-66.

Ots Capdequí, José María, 1934. Instituciones sociales de la América española en el periodo colonial. La Plata, Argentina: López.

Peña, Enrique A., 1935. Fragmentos históricos sobre temas coloniales dejados por Enrique Peña. Buenos Aires: Angel Curtolo.

Pereyra, Carlos, 1920-27. Historia de la América española. Madrid: "Saturnino Calleja." 8 vols.

Pino Manrique, Juán del: 1780. Informe del protector de naturales del Paraguay sobre encomiendas, dado por orden de la real audiencia, de resultas del que hizo al rei, D. Agustín Fernando de Pinedo, siendo gobernador de esta provincia. In Lamas, 1849, pp. 457-65.

Ramírez de Quiñona, Pedro: 1566. Carta a S. M. del Presidente de la Audiencia de Charcas, licenciado Pedro Ramírez de Quiñona. La Plata, 10 de noviembre. In Levillier, 1918, 1:204-13.

Ramírez de Velasco, Juán: 1597. Ordenanzas dadas por el gobernador D. Juán Ramírez de Velasco, sobre el gobierno y trato de los indios, 1 de enero. In García Santillán, 1928, pp. 356-75, Appendix.

Rubio, Julían María, 1942. Exploración y conquista del Río de la Plata. Siglos XVI y XVII. Buenos Aires: Salvat Editores.

Ruiz de Montoya, Antonio, 1892. Conquista espiritual hecha por los religiosos de la Compañía de Jesús en las provincias del Paraguay, Paraná, Uruguay y Tapé. Bilbao: Imprenta del Corazón de Jesús.

Salazar, Juán de: 1556. Carta de Juán de Salazar al Consejo Real de Indias, dando cuenta de sú expedición al Paraguay, y pidiendo, como primer poblador, que se le concediese a perpetuidad cierto numero de indios. Asumpción, 20 de marzo. In Cartas de Indias, 1877, 1:579-82, Document XCVIII.

Salmerón de Heredía, Juán: n.d. Memoria de Juán Salmerón de Heredía a S. M. In Garay, 1899-1901, 1:232-38.

Sánchez Valderrama, Pedro: 1612. Carta de Pedro Sánchez Valderrama, teniente de gobernador en la Asunción, sobre la inquietud de los indios a consequencia de la visita del licenciado Alfaro. Habla de lo ocurrido después de la salida de Hernan Arias de Saavedra. Asunción, 20 mayo. In Gandía, 1939, pp. 463-65, Appendix, Document XXVI.

Simpson, Lesley Byrd, 1929. The Encomienda in New Spain. Forced Native Labor in the Spanish Colonies, 1492-1550. Univ. Calif. Publ. in History, Vol. XIX.

_____, 1934. Studies in the Administration of the Indians in New Spain. Part I: The Laws of Burgos. Part II: The Civil Congregation. Ibero-Americana, No. 7.

_____, 1938a. Studies in the Administration of the Indians in New Spain. Part III: The Repartimiento System of Native Labor in Spain and Guatemala. Ibid., No. 13.

_____, 1938b. New Lamps for Old in Latin America. In: The Civilization of the Americas. Berkeley: Univ. Calif. Press.

_____, 1940. Studies in the Administration of the Indians in New Spain. Part IV: The Emancipation of the Indian Slaves and the Resettlement of the Freedmen. 1548-53. Ibero-Americana, No. 16.

_____, 1946. Many Mexicos. New York: G. P. Putnam's Sons.

Solórzano Pereira, Juán de, 1930. Política indiana. Madrid and Buenos Aires: Compañía Ibero-americana de publicaciones. 5 vols.

Steward, Julian H., 1943. Anthropological Research Needs and Opportunities in South America. Acta Americana, 1:20-37.

_____, 1945. The Changing American Indian. In Ralph Linton (ed.), The Science of Man in the World Crisis. New York: Columbia Univ. Press. Pp. 282-305.

_____, (ed.), 1946-50. Handbook of South American Indians. Bur. Amer. Ethnol., Bull 143. 6 vols.

Techo, Nicolás del, 1744-46. The History of the Provinces of Paraguay, Tucumán, Río de la Plata, Paraná, Guairá, and Urvaica. In Churchill, Awnsham (comp.), A Collection of Voyages and Travels. London: Printed by assignment from Messrs. Churchill, for H. Lintot, 4:680-807.

Téllez de Escobar, Diego: n.d. Relación de las cosas que han pasado en la provincia del Río de la Plata, desde que prendieron al governador Cabeça de Vaca. In Garay, 1899-1901, 1:260-72.

Torre Revello, José, 1943. Esteco y Concepción del Bermejo, dos ciudades desaparecidas. Buenos Aires: J. Peuser.

Trinidad, Antonio de la: 1556. Carta de Antonio de la Trinidad al Consejo de Indias, 2 de julio. In Garay, 1899-1901, pp. 227-30.

Vásquez de Espinosa, Antonio, 1942. Compendium and Description of the West Indies (trans. by Charles Upson Clark). Smithsonian Misc. Coll., Vol. 102.

Wagley, Charles, and Eduardo Galvão, 1946. O Parentesco Tupí-Guaraní. Bol. do Museu Nacional, nova serie, n. 6. Rio de Janeiro.

Washburn, Charles A., 1871. The History of Paraguay. Boston: Lee and Shepard. 2 vols.

Zavala, Silvio, 1943. New Viewpoints on the Spanish Colonization of America. Philadelphia: Univ. Pa. Press.

_____, 1946. Apuntes históricos sobre la moneda del Paraguay. El Trimestre económico, 13, No. 1:126-43.

www.ingramcontent.com/pod-product-compliance
Lightning Source LLC
LaVergne TN
LVHW050022250826
846302LV00008B/60